Both Sides Now

A Mother's Heavenly Perspective and a Daughter's Earthly One

Jennifer Marino

Book Cover painting by Judi Lakin
Graphic Design by Lorayne McGovern

ISBN: 978-1-64184-405-5 paperback
ISBN: 978-1-64184-406-2 ebook

Acknowledgements

First of all, I want to thank the maker and creator of the universe who has been with me every day through life's valleys and peaks. I want to thank my mother who I feel has truly collaborated with me on this book in Spirit. It was an honor to spend so much time with you. I want to thank the love of my life, my husband who has encouraged me gently to keep writing my story. I love you so much. I want to thank my sister from another mother for giving me the tools to write. You are the wind beneath my wings. Broken at one time, now soaring to new heights because of you. I want to thank my dear friend and riding buddy for painting the most magnificent book cover. It still takes my breath away. I want to thank my friends and family for all their support. I couldn't have revealed so much about myself without your encouragement. I also want to thank my editors who have helped mold and shape my manuscript. Last but not least, I want to thank myself. It wasn't easy to revisit every corner of my life, but it was so healing. I am a better person for having invested the time in myself.

BLESSED!

Prologue

A Mother's Heavenly Perspective

Looking back on my life, I wonder why I waited so long to release my spirit into the arms of God. There are no limits to what I can do from this incredible vantage point. I felt powerless in my earthly body, whereas in my spiritual body, I am the person I hoped to be.

I vacillated for years about whether to leave my husband. My family wanted me to, and even my kids urged me to get out. But I couldn't break a promise I made to God or to my husband. Things were very different in the fifties and sixties.

My father immigrated from Scotland in 1919 when he was twenty-one years old. My maternal grandmother left Ireland for America at the turn of the century. They were devout Roman Catholics who expected the same from their children. My father, an outstanding musician, was also a great textile dyer until he lost his sight at 36. When he was no longer able to work in textiles, he turned to music to make ends meet. Being the oldest child, I was the apple of his eye. I could do no wrong. My mother was an accomplished pianist who inspired me throughout my childhood with songs that flowed effortlessly from her precious heart onto the keys of our piano. I sat on the bench next to her and would sing along, hoping that one day I could play the piano like she did. She began teaching me to play when I was 8 years old. By the time I was 15, I became our church organist. I was proud to be entrusted with such an honor, but I also felt I was living my parents' life. I didn't want to disappoint them or God. Dad played every instrument known to man, but his favorites were the banjo and accordion. I accompanied him on the piano when friends and family visited. It wasn't long before Dad took our little show on the road to small community centers and to whomever would listen, which was everyone in those days. Music came alive in many peoples' home as it always had been in ours. We would play and sing our favorite songs for hours. I remember the first show we were supposed to do as if it were yesterday. I played the organ at the 8 a.m. Mass that Sunday, December 7, 1941. The Monsignor made an announcement that Japan had launched an attack on our Naval Base at Pearl Harbor in Honolulu. After Mass we went to our local community center. Everyone was so upset that our country was under attack. The music we played helped ease our distress.

What a magical childhood I had! My mother and father made me feel like anything was possible. My dad taught me to dream. I wasn't a natural dreamer, but with my dad's urging, I dreamed that I would one day be on Broadway! I wanted to make him proud. When I was seventeen, my younger sister Florence and I took the train to New York City. We wanted to be like the Lennon Sisters! She was beautiful, and I was, too, with dark brown hair and piercing blue eyes. We could also sing. How could we go wrong? There was an audition in New York City advertised for singers and dancers in our local newspaper. Dad urged us to go. When we failed to impress the judges at the audition, I would not be stopped. I reminded my sister that we passed the Ford Modeling Agency on our way to the audition. So, we paraded down there and worked our charm to land a face-to-face interview. Sadly, nothing came of our trip to New York City. Nothing except that my sister Florence and I became the closest of friends and confidantes.

We lived in a predominately French-speaking part of Massachusetts. When faced with the choice of French or English-speaking schools, Dad said, "Mary, you must learn the language of the land to succeed here." No one ever dared question Dad. I loved my father, but I felt I had to live my life for him. I excelled in school, as I did in all my pursuits. I was fascinated with French culture — so classy and refined compared to American culture, which was simple and unsophisticated.

When World War II ended in 1945, it was a time of great celebration in our hearts and homes. I had grown restless working in our little general store Mom set up in our home when Dad lost his sight. I wanted to go to college, perhaps. I took a job in my early twenties at a department store. One of the head buyers was a French-Canadian woman named Annette DuBois. She was the epitome of sophistication. She was what I aspired to be — a modern woman capable of anything. She had it all. She was a fine dressmaker, a career woman, and part of high society.

When I realized that my new boss, Annette, was as impressed with me as I was with her, I was excited about my promising future! She was a member of the most elite group in our community. I thought my perfect French and our mutual admiration would open doors and lead to incredible business opportunities. Little did I know, she had other plans for me; she thought I would make a great wife for her son, Jean. I had to wait to meet him because he was away at an

Ivy League school. I was so excited about the prospect of a college man.

Annette invited me to her home for dinner when Jean was home from school. When I walked in the door, I was astounded by the elegance of her home, such beautiful French Provincial furnishings and fine china. And Jean was handsome, confident, and charming. He swept me off my feet. He was in his last year of college at Brown University in an aeronautical engineering program — clearly brilliant. I was enchanted by the lovely dinner.

After our meal, Jean gathered the steak bones from our plates and took me out to the barn. The hunting dogs greeted us enthusiastically, jumping up to get Jean's treats. He quickly fed them the bones before they knocked him over. Clearly, he had a strong bond with them. They followed us into the barn, settled into a pile of soft hay, and happily gnawed on their bones.

The barn, twice as big as the house, had a large open hay loft with a ladder. Jean effortlessly raced up the ladder, while I looked on, admiring his athletic build. He tossed some hay down from the loft and sped down the ladder. We both grabbed bundles of hay to feed the horses. I thought the house was incredible, but the sight of these beautiful heavenly creatures was magnificent. We fed his black stallion named Tiny Tim and his white mare, Rose. He said Rose was Tiny Tim's girlfriend. They had a foal who was in the stall with his mother. It was so adorable — black with white spots on it with a pink little nose. Jean lit up when he was with them. He said when he was home from school, he spent all his time here. I asked him if he would take me for a ride someday.

He said, "What about tomorrow after you get home from church?"

I said, "That sounds great!"

"Rose is well-mannered, like you. You can trust her."

I peered at Rose and said, "I trust you," and then gazed at Jean and smiled.

Rose nudged my hand with her velvet nose. My heart felt so full. What I liked best about Jean was his love for animals. I had always felt sad that I wasn't allowed to have any as a child.

Whenever we asked our father if we could have a pet, his response was, "We have enough mouths to feed. We don't need anymore." I hoped Jean liked kids as much as he liked his animals. I wanted lots of children!

The next day he picked me up after church and we drove in his convertible sports car back to his home. The sun was shining. He had one hand on the steering wheel and one arm draped over my shoulders. I felt so free with the wind blowing in my hair and the sun on my face. The road to his house was lined with towering oak trees. There was a beautiful wooden three-rail fence around the long driveway with a huge pasture on each side of the property.

He saddled up Rose and Tiny Tim. Luckily, I had ridden boarding horses in my youth. One summer I even took hunter-jumping classes and learned to jump over small obstacles. Rose was an absolute doll, sweet and perfectly trustworthy. Tiny Tim, on the other hand, was full of himself, like Jean. He took me riding in the woods around their home. I had never had so much fun and excitement in my heart, as I did that day.

I said, "There must be horses in heaven."

He was puzzled. "Why do you say that?"

"Because the bible says the Lord, comes back to get us on a white horse like Rose."

He laughed. "You remind me of Rose."

I chuckled. "You remind me of Tiny Tim."

We ran the horses through the swaying green grass and the wildflowers gracing the pasture. I couldn't have imagined a more romantic adventure. I felt we were destined to be together. I knew he felt it, too, especially when my phone started ringing off the hook.

My dad said it was disrespectful for Jean to court me without first meeting my family and getting their blessing. I knew it was time to make introductions, but I was a little nervous. I reassured myself; Jean was from a sophisticated family, so he would know how to behave.

I couldn't have been more wrong. Jean was on his worst behavior. He sat in front of Dad, his feet perched on our coffee table, with a cocky, defiant attitude. What was he trying to prove? Later, I realized he was trying to show that he didn't need Dad's approval. It was too late though — I was madly in love.

He asked me to marry him and I said yes, of course. Annette said that all the gals in Paris were wearing custom-made suits instead of wedding dresses and that she would make mine. I was going to be married in style! It was time for me to break with tradition and stand up for myself for a change. My family was heartbroken. Being the oldest daughter, of course they assumed I would wear a white wedding dress, a veil, and have a big wedding. The fact that I wasn't planning to follow tradition was unheard of for a devout Catholic family. White symbolized purity and the Mother Mary.

We married the day after Christmas, December 26, 1949 in a small chapel near his house. After the service, Annette hosted us at her home for a formal sit-down dinner. I was so happy, yet my parents were so sad. It broke my heart that they weren't happy for me.

I realized later that I had married my father — a man no one would question. My mother loved my dad and was happy to sit back in silence. Although I had a few of Dad's characteristics, I had more of my mother's, like not speaking up to my dad until then. I wanted to be me for a change.

As newlyweds, we lived on campus until Jean graduated. I loved being a part of an academic community. I had always dreamed of going to college. But, sadly, it was not in the cards. I became pregnant with my first child, a boy, born in September 1950. I thought Jean would share in my happiness, but instead he was angry. That's when Jean's temper tantrums started. He didn't want to share me with anyone, especially not a child. He said he never wanted children. And incidentally neither did his mother, a career woman who didn't have time for them. When he was born, she hired a French nanny to care for him. When he was school-aged, he was shipped off to Catholic boarding school. Quite often, he could not even come home for Thanksgiving or Christmas. His mother couldn't be bothered with a child in the house while entertaining guests. It was no surprise that he hated holidays. When his classmates went home for the holidays, he was left alone at school. He told me he was essentially raised by Jesuit priests. One priest took advantage of the situation and molested him time and time again. It broke my heart to hear of such things. I finally understood the source of his torment.

I loved him so; I didn't believe in birth control and he was very passionate. It wasn't long before we had our second child, a girl. I was thrilled that our family was growing, but as it did, his fits of rage became more frequent. I loved my children and my husband. I didn't think I should have to choose. It was hard for me to see him so angry and the kids were frightened of him. They would hide in their room until things calmed down. This was the pattern for the next twenty years and the next five children. When he would fly off the handle, I would let them run to their rooms while I sat and listened to Jean scream. What more could I do? My family pleaded with me to leave him several times.

I said to my sister, "I choose to be happy, so be happy for me."

I got what I wanted. My husband did not. In time my family grew to accept it and stopped urging me to leave. Over the years my kids begged me to leave him, but it was against my faith to divorce my husband. And I loved him dearly.

He was a selfish man. We had seven children, and he chose to drive a little sports car that allowed for just one passenger. I drove a station wagon. Jean usually played tennis or went sailing on the weekends. The kids and I were happy to enjoy each other without his explosions. Sunday was his day to relax and unwind without us. I would gather the kids and we were off to church. My oldest son got the brunt of Jean's wrath. Jean was so jealous of him. He felt he lost me to him, and in a way, he did.

In July of 1968 when my youngest was four years old and my oldest seventeen, Jean got a job offer in California. We packed up the kids in the station wagon and set off for the West Coast. My family was crushed; they were inconsolable the day we left. To be honest, I was afraid that California would be too far away from my family. The sixties were a time of revolution in social norms — clothing, music, drugs and schooling. In 1964 segregation and discrimination were outlawed. It was a time of rebellion. I was rebelling, too, by moving so far away from my family and breaking their hearts. My eldest son enlisted in the Vietnam War in 1968. Why would someone volunteer to fight a losing battle so far away? Because it was better than fighting a losing battle at home. He felt he could never measure up to his father. Jean was harsh and never showed him any love. It broke my heart that I couldn't protect my son from the tyrant in our midst. He was tortured mentally, and all I could do was stand by and watch. What a coward I had become. Why couldn't I stand up to this man? Because I truly loved him and understood why he was so tormented.

I stayed by Jean's side despite his shortcomings. And now at 48, I cannot hang on any longer. Ovarian cancer courses through my body, and I don't have much time. I've prayed tirelessly for the peace I now feel. I hope I can better care for my kids from Heaven than from Earth. It's Thanksgiving Day, 1974; the time has come to release my Spirit into the welcoming arms of God.

Chapter One

Reunited

I have never felt such peace. I am weightless, like a ship at night, drifting; the current pulls me one way and then the other, rocking me back and forth. The night sky is like black velvet with diamonds scattered on it. A massive bright star is moving toward me. I'm transfixed by its beauty. It's getting brighter and brighter, as if it's illuminating my soul. I close my eyes and surrender. A warmth radiates from inside my heart. I am wrapped in a soft white cashmere blanket, as if cradled in my mother's arms. Like a swing in the summer breeze, I am swaying back and forth; I hear a lullaby being softly sung with the lovely instrumentals of a piano. Where have I heard that sweet melody before? Why, it's "Brahms' Lullaby."

Lullaby, and good night, in the skies, stars are bright. May the moon's silvery beams bring you sweet dreams. Close your eyes now and rest, may these hours be blessed. 'Til the sky's bright with dawn, when you wake with a yawn. Lullaby, and good night, you are mother's delight....

Deep in slumber, I imagine a place far away. I see in my mind's eye that it's so tranquil. Serenity washes over me. I am drifting deeper and deeper into a blissful dream.

The brilliant white light continues moving toward me — or am I moving toward it? I am floating, levitating. It's exhilarating to be this free and filled with such peace. Is this what happens when we die? Am I in heaven or between heaven and earth? Down below, I can see my life on Earth unfolding. My beautiful, sweet husband keeps me company in the hospital room. I love him so much. I wish he were here with me. I want to go to him, but I also want to let go. I trust God will lead me into this wondrous place. I am not afraid.

I ascend toward the luminescent light, drifting slowly upward. The scene of me lying in the hospital bed hooked up to a heart monitor while my dear husband sits vigil is getting farther and farther away. As I drift deeper into a new place of consciousness, the brilliant light transforms into a glorious doorway. I don't ever want to awaken from this euphoric dream state.

I leave my earthly body behind and float through an iridescent golden archway. The intense light is shining into my soul and emanating from my heart into the universe. It feels so warm and light, so effortless to drift like a feather in a gentle breeze toward the sun. I am a newly created spiritual being. I sense someone holding my hand, guiding me. I'm surrounded by love, as if many souls are touching me. Are they my spirit guides? Are they angels? Whoever they are, I know I'm in a sacred place.

I feel a presence and suddenly realize my eyes are closed. How is it possible to see such a bright light so clearly? I hesitate to open my eyes, afraid that when I do, I will leave this tranquil place. But my heart nudges me to see what's before me. Slowly opening my eyes, I see what I've yearned to see for so long — my mother standing next to me with her hand in mine.

"Hello, Jackie," she says in a voice so familiar.

"Mom?"

I am overcome with love and emotion and filled with unimaginable joy, yet this moment is bittersweet. It has been so long since I've felt her next to me. She gazes into my eyes and her face lights up. Her eyes melt away any doubt that we are together. She is such a lovely being. There's no question that I'm peering into her beautiful baby-blue eyes. Tears stream down her face and mine as we hold each other tight. I never want to let her go.

I feel more alive than ever, and peace fills my heart and soul.

"Come with me. I want to show you something."

She takes my hand in hers and leads me to a sacred garden with a magnificent, ancient oak tree, its roots twisting and turning deep beneath the transparent soil. I can see the faces of my husband, kids, siblings, father and mother in the branches and my relatives who have passed away are in the roots under the holy ground. Beneath this mighty oak tree is an exquisite dark wood bench with fine decorative carvings. We sit down and face each other, and I feel her heart and soul loving me. I fear if I take my eyes off her, she will disappear. I've missed her so much. I used to deny spiritual beings, but I have no doubt I am here with her now.

The sun's rays warm us. Birds chirp a symphony of love songs just for us. A sweet scent of fragrant roses fills the air. I've never known such happiness.

She says, "I was powerless from Earth and couldn't help you the way I wanted to. It was so hard for me to leave you. I love you so much and will never stop loving you. I couldn't hang on anymore. I had to let go of my spirit and trust God would take care of you. I hope you know I would have stayed with you if I could, Jackie, but I couldn't bear it anymore." Tears flow down her face, glistening like the sun shining on waves. She takes my face in her hands, looks deeply into my eyes and says, "I couldn't stay."

"I know you couldn't Mom. I wish you would have said good-bye or even left me a letter. It was so hard to live without you. I made some awful mistakes. I just wanted to self-destruct. I stopped loving myself and everyone else, so I didn't have to feel anymore. It hurt too much."

"I know. I have been with you always, even if you couldn't feel my presence."

I felt ashamed that she had been with me while I did so many awful things.

She reads my mind. "Don't be ashamed, Jackie. You did your best. I wanted to help you, but I had to trust that God would take care of you. It was so hard for me to watch you when you were in such unthinkable places. I'm sorry you had to endure those experiences without me to comfort you. I couldn't be with you in body, but I was always with you in spirit, Jackie. I know you couldn't feel me. I know it was too painful for you. Do you feel me now?"

"Yes, I do. I've waited so long to see you. I've missed you so much. I am so happy we are finally together." I gaze into her eyes, deep as the ocean. Her love is as wide as the universe. She peers into my soul. My heart is so full of love; it is overflowing. "I never want to leave."

She smiles. "I know, but it's not your time yet. You must return to your life and your loving husband. You must love him the way God intended before those awful things happened to you."

I am taken aback. I don't understand what is happening. "Haven't I died? Aren't I in heaven with you now?"

She peers deeply into my eyes. "No, Jackie, you haven't died, and we aren't in heaven. We are between worlds. I want to stay here with you, but it's time for me to go to the place God has prepared for me in heaven. And for you to return to the place He made especially for you on Earth. But to be released from the coma, you must revisit your life, learn from your mistakes, then let them go. Only then will you create the life you were meant to live."

"I want to stay with you. I...."

"I will never leave your side." She cradles my face with her soft featherlike hands and goosebumps run down my spine when she says, "Promise me that you know I will always be with you."

I peer deeply into her beautiful eyes and see the fluttering of gold iridescent butterfly wings. The translucent wings shine brightly in her eyes. Her tears, like a waterfall of our memories, flow from her heart and cleanse my soul.

I say, "I promise. I felt you so many times before, but I couldn't believe it was you. I couldn't bear the pain, so I dismissed it. I won't forget the time we've had here. Nothing can keep us from being together in spirit."

She takes my hand in hers. "It's time for me to go, Jackie."

"Can't we stay here just a little longer?" Tears cascade down my cheeks. I taste the salt and see my mother and me at the seashore when I was a child. We're digging in the sand on a sunny day. Sandpipers scamper down the beach and seagulls soar overhead. It's as if it were yesterday.

A vibrant yellow-and-black butterfly flutters and lands on the bench between us.

My mother says, "When you return to your life and spot a yellow butterfly, know that it's me. Wherever you go, please remember that I am with you and that I love you."

We stand and embrace. I don't want to let her go, but I know she is right. Living without her was hard but letting go now is even harder. Reluctantly, I release her. When I do, the butterfly spreads its wings, takes flight into the bright sky, and vanishes. She is gone.

Once again, I see myself lying on a hospital bed in a coma. There's a lovely bouquet of spring flowers on my bedside table and my husband is holding my hand. Nurses pop in and out of my room, checking my vitals and monitors, comforting my husband.

From this heavenly perspective, I can see the beginning of my life coming into view. It's as if I'm watching a movie, each scene being played out in front of me, as if it were happening right now. I lie motionless, thinking: ***As difficult as it is to look at my life, I must if I want to live the life of my dreams.***

A DAUGHTER'S EARTHLY PERSPECTIVE

CHAPTER TWO

SIX YEARS OLD

Most of our relatives live in Rhode Island. Dad always drives us there from our home in Connecticut, whether he wants to go or not.

"Get in the car, or you can stay home," he barks. I scramble into the far backward-facing seat of the station wagon, followed by my little sister Meagan, who is four (two years younger than I), and my older brother Paul, who is eight. The other siblings squeeze into the middle seat: Daniel (18), Laurie (16), Patty (13) and Debbie (11). It's like we have two different generations of siblings. I'm not very close to my older sisters and brother.

Dad and Mom sit in the front. Dad always smokes a pipe when he drives.

Both my mom and dad come from big families. Mom has shoulder-length dark brown hair and piercing blue eyes. Even without make-up, she's beautiful and always smiling or laughing. Dad is tall and thin with dark brown hair and brown eyes. He's good-looking, but, unlike Mom, he doesn't smile much. Dad went to Ivy League schools and is an aeronautical engineer at Pratt Whitney. Mom wanted to go to college, but it wasn't in the cards with so many kids. She attended a French-speaking high school and became fluent. Dad was born in Montreal, so English is his second language. They speak French when they don't want us kids to know what they are talking about. Mom says something to him in French as we drive away.

We are playing a game where we look out of the windows, searching for things. Whoever spots the thing we're looking for first wins that round — not that we're keeping exact score. But the one who's the best at spotting things gloats. If they get too cocky, we rib them. We are laughing, pointing, and challenging each other's claims.

"Cow," says Meagan.

I shout, "Over by the barn!" I'm proud of myself because I'm not always the best at finding stuff.

"Shut up! Why can't you all just shut up?!" Dad yells. In a fit of fury, he hurls his pipe out the window. We all freeze in silence. He jerks the car over to the side of the road and gets out to look for his pipe. As he disappears into the woods, I wonder what he is doing. I think he'd like to run away from us. I don't know what we've done to make him so mad. Maybe it's nothing we've done. Perhaps he was just born mad. Time stands still and I secretly hope he never comes back. I wish mom would drive away without him. He emerges from the woods with a stern expression, but no pipe. He climbs into the car and continues to drive, as if nothing has happened, as if he didn't just have a temper tantrum. He's driving mad — which means a little too fast for Mom's taste, but she doesn't say anything, to keep the peace. For the last hour of our trip, no one says a word for fear dad will blow up. It feels as if the air in the car is sucked out and we're suffocating. When it gets this bad, I want to throw my door open, hurl myself out onto the road, and run away. But I want to see my Grandpa and Grandma. They will make me feel better.

My maternal grandfather is from Scotland and speaks with a brogue. When he was a boy, he lost his eyesight in one eye while playing Three Musketeers with his best friend and using sticks as swords. Over time, he lost his sight in his other eye when he was 36, so he has never seen me with his eyes. When we walk into his home, he gets up from his seat at the head of a long white Formica table and gives me the biggest hug. I detect a faint smell of moth balls on his tweed wool blazer. He uses his hands, ears, nose, but mostly his heart, to get a sense of me by tracing my eyes and nose with his hands.

In his thick accent he says, "Jackie, you are such a pretty girl." If you don't know him, you might struggle to understand what he is saying. But listening to him speak is music to my ears. Grandma puts her hands on our cheeks and give them a little squeeze with her fingers, looks right into our eyes, and says, "You are such a tweetie-weetie." She makes me feel so loved. She does this to each one of us, but it doesn't make it any less special. We laugh about it later, but we love that we're all her tweetie-weeties.

Grandpa says, "Sit down and tell me what you've have been up to, Jackie." It doesn't matter what I say, he always replies enthusiastically, "That's wundaful, Jackie." He looks right at me with his gray cloudy eyes and his large Celtic nose and gives me a heartfelt smile. In that moment, I feel right down to my soul that I am the most important person in the world to him. I wish my father would make me feel this special. Around him I feel worthless. My mother's parents don't show him much love. They think their daughter could've found a man who was a better husband and father but are glad that he's at least Catholic.

I wear cat-eyeglasses and my older sister's hand-me-downs. It doesn't seem fair that just because we're younger, Meagan, Paul, and I are stuck wearing worn-out duds when the older kids get brand-new clothes. The only time I get something new is if Mom makes it for me. Being a talented seamstress, she sometimes makes matching dresses for my little sister and me. I feel stupid wearing the same dress as Meagan, but I don't let Mom know, since she puts so much time and love into it. She says I look like Jackie O, the First Lady, my namesake. She loves Jackie O and President Kennedy. Mom told me he was assassinated when I was younger.

We gather around the table while Grandma puts on the tea kettle. She lines up thick pink plastic teacups stained from years of use on the light green Formica counter. She carefully drops a tea bag into each cup. While she waits for the kettle to whistle, she toasts cinnamon raisin bread and places it on a dinner plate. The scent of cinnamon is making my mouth water. She takes small glasses that look like Welches Grape Jelly jars out of the cupboard and pours the kids ginger ale.

While we wait for Grandma to serve us, Grandpa asks each one of us what we've been up to and always has the same reply: "That's wundaful."

I love the sound of the kettle whistling, like a train coming down the tracks. Grandma fills each cup with piping hot water and places one in front of Grandpa, Mom, and my older brother and sisters. I can't wait until I'm old enough to have a cup of tea.

Grandma sits down next to Grandpa and puts three heaping teaspoons of sugar and lots of milk in Grandpa's cup and passes the sugar and milk to Mom. She sees me slathering my toast with lots of butter and passes me the sugar. I smile, put a spoonful on my toast, and take a bite. The cinnamon, raisins, but mostly the sugar, taste like heaven inside my mouth. Grandma sits contentedly with a peaceful grin as Mom and Grandpa catch up on the latest news. Very charismatic and opinionated, Grandpa does most of the talking. You don't argue with him; he always gets the last word in. Maybe that's why Mom is okay with Dad. She learned from her dad that some things are better left unsaid. I've also learned it doesn't pay to argue. It only makes things worse and sets Dad off. I argue with him in my mind, though. And maybe one day I'll get up the nerve to stand up to him and not care if he flies off the handle into a rage. What's the worst that could happen?

After tea and toast, we file into the living room for a little music — one of my favorite family traditions. Grandpa plays every instrument known to man, including the bagpipes. Mom plays the piano and Grandpa plays the banjo. We sing, "Won't You Come Home, Bill Bailey." Dad escapes to the sunporch to have a cigarette.

On the piano are eight pictures of Grandma and Grandpa's kids, from oldest to youngest, in connected, hinged brass frames. Mom's is the first one on the left because she's the oldest. In the living room Jesus and Mother Mary statues stand in the bay window. When Mom and Grandma pass them, they give the sign of the cross. But not Dad; he hates religion. He was raised by Jesuit priests at an all-boys boarding school. He wasn't allowed to go home on the holidays. His parents were entertaining guests and they couldn't be bothered by a boy at the table. I heard Mom telling my older brother and sisters that Dad was abused by a priest. Perhaps that's why he hates church and ruins every holiday. On holidays we kids remain quiet as mice at the table or he will explode. It's no wonder I dread the holidays. Instead of having fun and celebrating, like other families, I feel as if I am walking on eggshells; one wrong word or action away from dad going ballistic.

But I'm lucky in one respect. I can't imagine a better grandfather and grandmother. Grandma is the sweetest woman in the whole wide world. She has beautiful baby-blue eyes, like Mom, and a dainty little smile. She always wears a cotton house dress with floral patterns, perhaps because she is a little heavy-set and it is more comfortable than an ordinary dress. I sit next to her on the brown mohair couch, which is itchy, but I don't mind because I'm with Grandma. She takes my hand into hers and gives it a little squeeze. I squeeze her hand in return and smile up at her. I breathe in her fresh Ivory-soap scent and look at her light pink cheeks, which make her look like a doll. My mom has the same doll cheeks. Grandma taught Mom to apply lipstick and then smudge a little on her cheeks.

We are going to visit our cousins, who live on the other side of the woods behind our grandparents' house. My aunt and uncle have 12 kids—six girls and six boys. We run ahead while Dad smokes a cigarette. It's fun to charge through the woods like wild animals. Blackberries are in season, so we stop to pick some along the way. It is so magical to eat berries right off the bush. They taste so sweet in my mouth, but even sweeter in my soul. I wish I could stay here forever.

Paul, Meagan, and I are going with our mother and grandfather to a retirement home, so we only stay a short time. Dad is going to play tennis with our Uncle. My older siblings urge us to stay with them at our cousin's house to play, but my mom says, "Not today. We are scheduled to perform at the retirement home. We will pick you up after we take my father home later."

I'm torn. I wish we could stay and play with our cousins, because they are so much fun, but I also want to sing and dance for the old folks. After we quickly greet our aunt, uncle, and cousins, we run back to Grandpa and Grandma's house. We pick and gobble up more berries as we go. We play on the swing set, while Mom gets Grandpa settled in the station wagon. Paul, Meagan, and I jump in the backseat. Grandma never goes with us to the retirement homes. She's a homebody who prefers time alone. She stands in the driveway and waves until our car is out of sight. We kids are hanging out of the windows waving back at her. The so-called O'Leary wave is Grandpa and Grandma's tradition. Whenever anyone is leaving their home, they walk outside and wave to them as they drive away. We do the O'Leary wave at home, too, because I guess it's become our tradition, too.

When we arrive at the retirement home, we head straight for the cafeteria. The residents are sitting at the tables and milling about. I breathe through my mouth because it smells like liver and onions. Half-eaten plates are scattered around the cafeteria. The food looks so unappetizing: peas, burnt potatoes, and mystery meat. No wonder the residents didn't finish their meals.

We're setting up to perform for the residents. Mom places her score on the piano and Grandpa is getting situated with his accordion. Then it's show-time!

I dance and sing "Life is a Cabaret" like Liza Minnelli. I'm a little nervous, but, in truth, I love being the center of attention. The residents are smiling and swaying to our music. It is truly magical performing for people who enjoy my singing. I feel like a star and don't want it to end. The residents give me a standing ovation . Next, Paul plays boogie woogie on the piano. Everyone applauds enthusiastically. Meagan will sing "Me and My Shadow" by Liza Minnelli. She is nervous, but I give her a nudge and say, "You can do it!"

She does a great job, considering she forgets a few lines, but no one seems to notice. The seniors give her a hearty round of applause as she hurries back to her seat.

We drop Grandpa at his house, pick up Dad and the other kids at our Aunt and Uncle's house and head to dad's mom's house for dinner. I dread Sunday dinner because my grandmother is uptight and a stickler for proper behavior.

I never met my dad's father because he died before I was born. His mom was his father's second wife. We call her Mimi, which means Grandma in French. She is so proper and formal and makes me feel like I can't do anything right. I wonder if that is how she made my father feel growing up. She always corrects my table manners, saying things like, "Sit up straight," "Put your napkin in your lap," and "Don't put your elbows on the table." The worst part is she doesn't let us drink water or milk until we are done with our meal. I excuse myself to go to the bathroom where I take a big long drink of water from the faucet.

My dad's parents had him later in life when his half-siblings were out of the house. His father was a dentist and his mother, a socialite, was a buyer for a high-end department store. Being career-oriented, they didn't have time for him. Dad was shipped off to boarding schools when he was in grade school. Perhaps because he felt abandoned and unloved by his parents, my dad doesn't know how to love us kids. It seems we are just in his way. And I can tell he doesn't like all the attention we take from our mother. He cuts us off in the middle of a conversation with Mom. He often says, "Children are meant to be seen and not heard." What does he mean? When he says that, we speak when we are spoken to, no more and no less.

While Dad grew up in high society, my mom with devout Roman Catholic parents had a simple life. She was so fortunate to have two wonderfully loving parents. I wonder what that would be like. Sometimes it feels like Mom tries to smother us with love to make up for Dad's shortcomings.

All the kids except me fall asleep on our way home. I am just resting my eyes, listening to my parents talking.

"Jean, I know how hard it is for you to visit your mom. Thank you for going. I think it's important for the kids to know your mother."

My dad doesn't respond.

"I know how hard it was for you when you were younger," she says.

"I don't like to think about it," he says quickly.

I can see they really love each other. Maybe that's why she doesn't stand up to him when he yells and screams. I open my eyes to see her lean over and kiss him on the cheek and then put her head on his shoulder and fall asleep. I nod off, dreaming of how it would be to be in love. I wish my dad loved us the way he loves our mother.

* * *

The next weekend, Mom takes us to the beach to go clamming after church. The beach is just five miles from Mystic Seaport, Connecticut, where we live. I breathe in the ocean air while watching the seagulls swoop down over the ocean to catch fish. The baby sandpipers are peeping as they scurry to keep up with their mother. She never looks back to make sure they're keeping pace.

Mom brought shovels and buckets for us to dig for clams. Mom is making clam chowder for dinner tonight, which everyone loves. The more clams, the better. My brothers, sisters, and I are digging holes in the sand near the ocean tide. When the waves come in, little bubbles appear where the clams are. We extract them from the sand and fling them into our buckets. We compete to see who wins at clamming. Since no one keeps exact count, it's always the person who brags the most.

Dad is out on his sailboat that he docks at the marina. He sails a lot and never takes us kids. We are too little, or so he says. He likes to go sailing to blow off steam — of which he has a lot. I don't know why he had so many kids if he doesn't want to spend time with us.

It's a beautiful sunny day, not a cloud in the sky. The nice steady breeze should make Dad happy, if that's even possible.

Mom doesn't have to load the chowder with potatoes because we gathered lots of clams. She doesn't work, so we are always trying to stretch our food by adding rice or potatoes to the recipe. My little sister, older brother, and I are running around the kitchen screaming, "I got more clams than you did."

"Keep it down," my older sister whispers. "Dad is resting before dinner."

Anxiety courses through me, but it's too late. A door slams in the other room. We all look like we've seen a ghost, as Dad charges into the kitchen yelling, "Can't I even get a little sleep around here? I work Monday through Friday and spend my weekends in Rhode Island with relatives. Isn't that enough?"

We remain silent. It's best to say nothing and to make yourself as small as possible.

Then he blurts, "Well, I am happy we are moving to California. I want to get the hell out of here!"

What is he talking about? We have heard nothing about California!

By the looks on our faces, he realizes Mom hasn't told us. He yells, "Go to your rooms!"

We spread out and run. We can hear Mom and Dad arguing in the kitchen. Paul, Meagan, and I head to our room. I don't mind sharing a room with Paul, because he makes me feel safe and secure. But Meagan and I fight a lot. She's always making wisecracks, which can be funny but annoying if you're not in the mood. Paul is more serious. He sometimes has the guts to stand up to Dad. We are trying to hear what Dad is saying to Mom. We whisper about Dad making us move to California. We don't want to move away from our wonderful, loving relatives.

I feel like my world is crumbling. I cry myself to sleep without dinner.

Looking back now on the move, I realize it broke my heart in two. Half of it stayed with my loving grandparents, aunts, uncle, and cousins. The other half went with my family to California. Those early memories on the East Coast would serve as a beacon of light and would show me the way out of the darkness that would soon come.

Chapter Three

Eight Going on Ten

We are at our aunt and uncle's house gathered on their wrap-around porch. We are visiting them one last time before we head to our new home in California. With mom's seven siblings and their spouses and kids here, we have so many people to say good-bye to. I can't imagine not having them in our lives anymore. Our aunts and uncles are telling stories of growing up with Mom. Meagan and I are on the porch swing, slowly swinging back and forth, wondering when we will see them again.

Dad stands by the car smoking a cigarette, when he blurts out, "Let's go. We have a long drive today."

As I hug my relatives, it's as if each hug pulls on my heart. I can barely stand up; my legs feel like they are giving way under the weight of my body.

Grandpa gives me a bear hug and senses me sobbing uncontrollably. He wipes the tears from my face, places his warm hands on my cheeks and looks at me with his cloudy gray eyes. I miss him already. He says, "You'll make lots of new friends in California, Jackie. Always remember that a stranger is a friend you haven't met, yet. You'll see."

I hope he is right, but I doubt it.

Staring out the back window of our station wagon, watching the rain fall onto the pavement, I look up at the sky and say in silence, *Why, God? Can you hear me?* There isn't an ounce of blue in the sky. The low gray clouds match our moods. Why do we have to leave everything familiar behind — my home, my relatives, my life? It isn't fair. I'm afraid of the unknown that lies ahead. Being the second to the youngest of seven kids, I feel lost in the crowd. In fact, I could disappear, and no one would notice. I am a passenger in their lives, just going along for the ride. Whether I want to or not, we are moving to California.

As we drive past rows of New England-style homes and dense trees to the wide-open highways, I let out a big sigh. My brother Paul looks at me and does the same. We've been on the road for hours. I am sleepy, so I rest my head on his shoulder and fall asleep. Suddenly, I wake up to my brother nudging me and notice everyone is getting out of the car.

We are at a rest stop with a Howard Johnson's restaurant. My dad is putting gas in the car while we get a table and use the bathroom. I'm worried about being here, as my dad always makes a scene in public. I don't want to rock the boat, so I sit quietly. I am always one of the last to order. While I wait for Mom, Dad, and my older brothers and sisters, a heavy-set, middle-aged, impatient waitress is waiting for me to decide what I want. I don't want to be a bother to anyone, so I order the cheapest thing on the menu — eggs, bacon, and toast for $1.99. I want the waffles for $3.99, but I don't want Dad to get mad. My little sister orders the same thing. No one says much while we eat our breakfast. As I eat my dry toast and burnt bacon, I imagine how delicious those waffles with sweet maple syrup would have been. It feels like we are all holding our breath. None of us wants to move to California , except our father. I think he wants to get as far away from our relatives as possible. I can tell he doesn't like them that much. If I said what I was thinking, my dad would blow up, so I don't say anything at all.

When we get back on the highway, I notice the homes don't look anything like those in Connecticut and Rhode Island. There aren't many trees, either. It is all so unfamiliar, and the unknown creeps back in, wondering what tomorrow will bring. Even though there are nine of us in the car, you could hear a pin drop. It's dead quiet. Dad likes it that way.

Dad pulls into a KOA campground. We all scramble to get our things to set up camp. We're planning to be on the road for three days and two nights. The older kids run to the showers. Mom tells us younger kids to put on our swimsuits and go to the lake while Mom and Dad set up the tent.

When we return to the campsite, it's dinner time, which is a good thing, because I'm starving. Dad orders us to find sticks to roast hotdogs. He found a few long branches and takes the small branches off it and places a few hot dogs on each one. He hands one to Mom. It's nice sitting around the fire roasting our hotdogs together.

When we polish off our hotdogs, it's late and we are zonked. Mom tells us to fetch our pillows and blankets from the car. The tent is a big green canvas military tent Dad scored at a garage sale. I can't sleep because the ground is hard as a rock. We younger kids set up our beds in the far back of the tent in the corner. I am wedged up against Meghan and Paul. My older brother and sisters are in the other corner next to us. Mom is making a bed out of blankets for Dad and her closer to the door. There's very little room to move. I need to pee, so I tiptoe over my brother and sister, trying not to step on them. I tell Mom I need to go to the bathroom. She tells me to hurry back. I climb over her and out the screen door. Dad is smoking his pipe by the fire.

He says, "What's the matter?"

"I need to use the bathroom."

He hands me a flashlight. I walk in the darkness with nothing but his flashlight guiding me. An owl hoots in the distance. It's a little spooky. I pick up my pace to the restroom and walk even faster back to our camp. When I get back, the fire is out, and Dad is in the tent. I tiptoe into the tent, lie down in the back corner, and fall asleep.

After breaking down the tent and packing up our things before dawn, it's good to be on the road again. We all tried to pitch in, but Dad made a stink about too many chiefs and not enough Indians, so we let Mom and Dad do it alone. I don't understand what he means, but I'm not about to ask. Mom made some peanut butter-and-jelly sandwiches for us to eat in the car. I didn't sleep much last night, so I crash after I scarf down my sandwich.

I wake up hours later, when everyone is getting out of the car at a gas station. I need to pee, so I hurry out of the car behind my brothers and sisters. Mom is buying some dinner at Kentucky Fried Chicken next to the gas station while we use the bathroom. She says, "Wash your hands, please." Mom and Dad are sitting at a large picnic table outside when we return. We never eat fast food. I am excited to try some. Dad and Mom each get a large chicken breast, the older kids each get a thigh and a wing, and the younger kids get chicken legs. It's so delicious; I wish I could have another piece.

I risk it. "I'm still hungry."

Dad says, "Fill up on bread. When you're a father, you can have a bigger piece," he says, chuckling. I don't find it funny, but I fake a laugh, so he doesn't get mad. I grab a piece of bread and slather butter on it. It's yummy.

We pile back into the car after dinner and keep driving west on Highway 40. It's late and we've been driving all day. Dad pulls into a Motel Six in Flagstaff, Arizona. He doesn't want to camp again. I'm relieved. The motel floor is a little softer than the ground. We have a television, too. From our beds on the floor, we watch *Chitty Chitty Bang Bang*, starring Dick Van Dyke, while Mom and Dad go to sleep in the bed.

The next day, as we drive out of Flagstaff toward California, I see signs for the Grand Canyon. I wish we could go there, but we are in a hurry to get to California, as Dad starts work in a few days. I almost say something, but then I think it's best to keep my thoughts to myself. For the rest of our journey west, we just stare out the windows and don't say much.

We arrive at the house Dad rented in Palos Verdes, California, on Sunday evening. I am exhausted, as I didn't sleep much on the motel-room floor. We all jump out of the car to go check out our new house. It's a single-level home that looks more modern than our home in Connecticut. The homes are closer together, too. There are four bedrooms and two baths. We can see the bedroom assignments by where the movers set up the beds. Meagan,

Paul, and I will share a room. Laurie, Patty, and Debbie will share another. Daniel gets his own room; it's the smallest. My mom and dad are in the master bedroom.

Dad drove his sports car here a week ago and met the movers, then flew back to Connecticut. I wish we could have flown here. I have never been on a plane. Mom said it only took Dad five hours to fly from California to the East Coast.

I'm glad to be out of the car — where we had to be quiet — and in our room with my sister and brother where we can talk. I don't have anything in common with my older siblings, but Paul, Meagan, and I are tight. My mom tells the older sisters they are in charge of us. She puts Laurie in charge of Paul, Patty in charge of me, and Debbie in charge of Meagan.

Mom says, "I want you to listen to your older sisters. Because we are new here and don't know anyone in the community, it is especially important that we look out for each other."

We are stepping around the boxes in our room, when Patty comes in and tells us to unpack them. We are tired, but glad we have something to do. Our bunkbed is set up on one side of the room and Paul's twin bed is on the other. Meagan has always had the upper bunk, because I don't like to have to climb up and down to go to the bathroom in the middle of the night. We just lie down on top of our bare mattresses and talk for a bit before we start unpacking.

School is out for the summer, so we have time to explore our new neighborhood. A big canyon out our backyard gate beckons us to play hide-and-seek and go for long hikes. We have an avocado tree in our backyard.

I've never tried one before. I like the taste and the creamy texture. We pick a bunch of them and put them in brown paper lunch bags to sell in our front yard to the neighbors.

Daniel joined the Marines shortly after we arrived in California. He is at boot camp in Camp Pendleton and will soon be sent to Vietnam. I am sad my oldest brother is going away. Even though Grandpa told me that a stranger is a friend I haven't met yet, I don't know how to make friends here. Maybe California kids are just different from East Coast kids. My older siblings are making more friends than we are.

On Saturday, Daniel is back from boot camp and has brought his buddies with him. They all have buzz haircuts. My sisters and their friends act giddy because Daniel's friends look so handsome in their uniforms. Their haircuts show off their good-looking faces, too. I think they are so cute.

We all sit in a circle in the front yard. The older kids let us younger kids hang out with them. Everyone except the Marines has long hair, including the guys who didn't go to boot camp. Some of them have hair all the way down to their butts. My hair has grown a lot more, too. I want to look like them. Meagan and I go around the circle, sitting behind the big kids and do their hair. For some of the girls, I do a braid. For others, I brush their hair. Paul gives them shoulder rubs. One of the guys begins playing the guitar and everyone sings "Hey, Jude" by the Beatles.

Mom brings out some beer. One of the guys passes around a hand-rolled cigarette. Everyone takes a puff, except for us little kids and Mom. Some of them cough as they blow out the smoke. It smells like a skunk — nothing like the cherry pipe tobacco my dad smokes. I wonder why they like it.

Mom says, "If they are old enough to go to war, they are old enough to drink beer."

Daniel says, "I would rather go to war than stay here fighting a losing battle with Dad."

I completely understand why Daniel wants to leave. Dad constantly puts him down, making him feel as if he can't do anything right. Dad's mom did that to me. I guess he learned that awful behavior from her.

I am sad he is going off to Vietnam in a few days. *Please, Lord,* I pray, *protect my brother and his friends and bring them back to us.*

Some of his buddies are talking about how they might not come home. One guy said his brother was killed in the war. My older sisters and their friends are crying. I can tell Mom is scared, too. I saw her crying earlier today when I walked into the living room. Dad and Mom were sitting on the couch listening to Beethoven, one of my dad's favorite composers. He usually listens to his music with headphones, so we don't disturb him.

Daniel's friend Dave gets up from the circle and begins passing around the beer to the other guys. Mom hurries back into the house. I can hear her playing "Both Sides, Now," by Joni Mitchell, on the piano and singing it so beautifully. She used to play more traditional folk songs she learned from Grandpa, but now she prefers songs of the '60s. I've memorized all the words to "Both Sides, Now" on Joni's "Clouds" album. The words ring so true to me. I feel it in my soul.

* * *

The school year flies by. I liked the first grade. My teacher, Mrs. Franklin, was so nice to me. I met some new friends, but I didn't invite them over, because I didn't want them to see how my dad behaves around kids.

I have learned to be seen and not heard. I also figured out how to be of service and to stay out of everyone's way. I help Mom in the kitchen, and when Dad gets home from playing tennis or sailing, I give him a back rub. He never hugs any of us kids or says, "I love you." I love him despite his yelling and screaming. I wish just once he would tell me he loves me like other kids' dads.

I am glad it's summer again, because swimming is one of my favorite things. We learned to swim back in Connecticut when Mom would take us to the community center in the summer. We would spend hours swimming while mom read her books on a lounge chair.

Mr. Wilson, the old man down the street, lets the neighborhood kids swim in his pool. There's a huge slide on the deep end; it's our favorite thing about the pool. There's nothing more fun than climbing to the top of the slide, sliding down, and plunging into the deep end. We sometimes get water up our noses, but we don't care. We swim to the side, jump out of the pool, and do it all over again.

Mr. Wilson reminds me of my grandfather. He looks a lot like him, too. He doesn't seem to have a wife, kids, or grandkids, though. He must be a lonely old man. He likes to hang out with us kids and gives us all the soda and candy we want. We never have soda at our house, unless someone is sick. A few times I even faked being sick just to get soda.

One day I'm having a blast playing with the neighborhood kids on the slide when Mr. Wilson pulls me aside. He asks me to come back later by myself. He says he has something to show me, which excites me. I like being around Mr. Wilson, because he makes me feel special, unlike my dad. With him I just feel like I'm in the way.

I tell Mom I am going out to play. She wants me to be home by dinner. When I arrive at Mr. Wilson's, his smile reveals discolored, stained teeth. I can tell he is happy to see me. He looks as old as my grandpa, his face wrinkled like a prune. I am not sure how old he is; I just know he's ancient.

"What do you want to show me?" I ask.

"Follow me," he says. He leads me into his bedroom. He claps his hands and the lights come on.

My face lights up like a Christmas tree.

"Do you want to try it?"

I nod. I clap my hands and the lights turn off. I notice a life-sized blow-up doll sitting in the chair next to his bed. "What is that?"

He chuckles. "It's my girlfriend."

I giggle. I think he is so funny.

"Do you want to play a game?"

"Sure! What kind of game?"

"I will be the baby kitten and you will be the momma cat." He pats the bed, indicating that I should climb up.

I walk closer and he lifts me onto the bed. He pulls my dress up and pulls down my panties. He begins to lick my private parts.

"You taste sweet like a lollipop," he says.

"It tickles." I laugh. I have never had someone touch me down there before. It kinda feels good, but I am very uncomfortable. It just seems wrong, but I'm not sure why.

After a few minutes, he pulls my panties up and my dress down and lifts me off the bed. "Did you like the kitten game?"

I don't know what to say. He has a creepy expression on his face. I feel a little afraid of him now, like maybe he shouldn't have done that to me. "I should go home now, or I'll be late for dinner."

"This is our special little secret. Don't tell anyone you were here. Okay?" He takes a big bowl from the coffee table filled with little lollipops with brightly colored wrappers. "Take one. Or what the heck, take two!"

"Okay." I pick orange and grape, although I'm not sure I should take any.

He says, "Promise?" and extends his pinky finger and wraps it around mine. I can't look him in the eyes, as he seems more than a little creepy now.

"Promise," I say while trembling; I run out the door.

On my way home, I wonder why I can't tell anyone I was there. *Did I do something wrong? Maybe I shouldn't have played kitties with him. No one has ever licked me down there.* I don't want to get in trouble, so I decide not to tell anyone about it. I unwrap the purple wrapper and pop the sucker into my mouth. It tastes delicious like grape soda.

When I get home, my mom asks me where I got my lollipop.

"Mr. Wilson gave it to me."

"What were you doing there?"

"Playing."

"Were you alone?"

"Yes."

She says firmly, "Don't go there alone anymore."

Maybe I shouldn't have told her I was there. I used to like how he made me feel special. Now he just seems like a creepy old man. I run to my room, throw myself onto the bed, and cry.

Paul comes in and lies down on his twin bed. "Where were you? We've been looking all over for you."

"None of your business." I roll over and close my eyes.

He walks out and slams the door.

I'll never tell my siblings or my parents that Mr. Wilson touched my private parts. I have a secret I can't tell a soul.

Little did I know then that I would keep that secret hidden deep in my heart for so long that it became a part of me. I remember feeling so much shame and remorse for going there. That's when I began to not trust men. I still hold on to a small part of that. Now that I am older and wiser, I think I know who I can trust and who I can't.

Chapter Four

Ten Going on Twelve

One night at dinner, Patty makes the mistake of asking Dad how his day was. He starts yelling and screaming and slamming his hands down on the table.

"Do you want to know how the hell my day was? Well, I lost my job! My boss is an asshole who thinks he knows everything!"

I can't believe he lost another job. Now what are we going to do?

Everyone is frozen as he yells at my sister. We know that intervening only makes it worse. There's no other way to say it: He is an awful father.

Everyone quickly finishes eating. My sister Patty gets up and puts her plate in the sink, so us kids follow her with our dishes and scurry to our rooms.

Meagan, Paul, and I are lying on our beds not saying a word. I am thinking, *why does Dad keeps losing his job? He must yell and scream at work, too. This is the second job he has lost in three years. Maybe that is what mom and he always argue about.* We can still hear him yelling at mom.

Dad found a job in Cincinnati at General Electric, thank God. I was worried he wouldn't find a new job and would be more upset that he must figure out how to take care of us. Daniel is still in Vietnam and I pray he is all right. Laura fell in love with a guy Patty once dated and moved into his house after Daniel went to war. Patty has been answering phones at a car dealership and moved into an apartment with friends. I wish my older brother and sisters were coming with us. Who knows when we will see them again? *Why, God, do you keep taking away the people I love?*

I am afraid to move again, but I am also relieved; I can leave the bad memories behind. And I don't have many friends to say good-bye to, as I've decided it's easier to be alone. It seems hopeless to make friends, because I don't want anyone to see what goes on here.

I am not looking forward to the trip to Ohio, as Dad is driving us there. He sold his sports car last week because we needed the money. We have packed up the station wagon and are on our way. There's a knot in my stomach and it's hard to breathe. I don't know how far Ohio is, just that it's going to take a few days to get there. Mom is in the front seat of our Vista Cruiser station wagon and we four younger kids are in the back. We are real quiet the whole way. The knot in my stomach feels like a huge rock.

Thank God it only takes a few days to get to Ohio. I can breathe again. We scurry out of the car to see the house Dad rented when he came here to interview a few weeks ago. It's much smaller than the house in California. It's a little three-bedroom, one-bath house. We don't need as many bedrooms now, with our older siblings living in California, but I can't believe the six of us have to share a bathroom. Paul, Meagan, and I will share a room and

Debbie gets her own room. It looks a lot like Connecticut here. There are a lot more trees and a lot less traffic than in California. Dad hates to sit in traffic. He didn't like driving in Los Angeles. Neither did we; it took forever to get anywhere.

* * *

During the day while we are at school, Mom writes short stories about her childhood that she submits to *Reader's Digest* contests. One story she published, "When the Camels Came" is about her family at Christmas and represents the Three Kings bringing gifts to Jesus at his birth. While in California, she also wrote a song for the church hymnal. It is called "The Oldest Little Child," referring to Jesus. Growing up, she was the church organist.

She goes to church every morning when she drops us off at school. I am going to a Catholic school now and am required to go to church every day. This is my first experience with Catholic school, and I'm not a huge fan. I much prefer public school, because we can wear our own clothes instead of an awful uniform — a gray and blue plaid skirt that hangs down to my knees and a white button-down blouse. Paul wears a uniform, too. He looks funny dressed in his knee-length gray and blue plaid shorts and a white dress shirt.

While we kneel in church, the nuns inspect us to make sure our skirts touch the ground. If they don't, they send us home to change. The girls at school bring masking tape in their backpacks to shorten their skirts at recess. I don't shorten mine, though. I don't want to be sent home.

Mom is a Good Samaritan who leads by example. One day on our way home from school, we spot a car accident. The car was left on the side of the road and there is lots of debris on the road. Mom pulls over and grabs the broom, dustpan, and orange cones permanently stored in the back of the car for when she sees glass on the road. She puts the cones out, so the cars will go around us. When I see a friend's mom driving my friend home from school, I duck. My brother and sister laugh at me. It's so embarrassing that Mom is the accident janitor, sweeping up glass on the road. This isn't the first time, and it won't be the last. She used to do it in Los Angeles, where there are a lot of car accidents.

Mom bakes us cookies to snack on before we do our homework. I love her oatmeal cookies with raisins and walnuts. She also makes cookies that look like dog poo, so I call them "poo poos." She mixes oatmeal, sugar and chocolate, forms cookies, and places them on wax paper on the counter. They are no-bake cookies that harden by sitting for a few hours. I snatch two before they're completely ready. I love the way the chocolate melts in my mouth, leaving the chewy oatmeal covered in sugar. I ask her if she will teach me how to make them. She promises she will. She taught me how to make the oatmeal cookies, which I love doing with her.

After we finish our homework, we go out to play. There are so many kids in our new neighborhood. It's a good thing, because our family is down to four kids. I'm envious of my older siblings getting to live on their own. I don't blame them. I hate living with Dad. But if I were to move out, I'd miss Mom like crazy. So, perhaps I'm not ready after all.

We sometimes get to do some fun stuff with Dad, like go to plays in the park. His company gives him free tickets. When we go, Dad stops by the stables in the park to see the horses. He says he will teach me to ride someday, but I know he won't. He never does anything he promises. But it's obvious Dad loves to be around horses. Mom tells us Dad grew up with horses and they would ride around his parents' property when they were dating. She fell in love with horses and Dad. We can see by the way they are talking that they remember Dad's horses, Tiny Tim and Rose. I've never seen them, but I've heard them talk about his horses many times. I, too, love horses!

Whenever we see horses on the side of the road, Mom stops so we can pet their soft noses. They feel like velvet and make me want to snuggle with them. Around horses, my heart feels warm and happy and I have butterflies in my tummy. Sometimes we bring them carrots and apples on our way home from school. Many homes in the neighborhood have big barns and beautiful pastures. Mom gives me toy plastic horses every year on my birthday. I like to name them and pretend that I have several horses all my own. I would like to own a horse someday.

Tonight, we are going to see the play *Oklahoma*. We get settled on our blanket in the park and the musical begins. I love watching the actors sing and dance and hope to do that one day. I know I'd enjoy acting like someone other than me. Meagan, Paul, and I dance to the music, laugh, and sing the songs Mom has taught us when she plays the piano. It reminds me of when we used to go to nursing homes with Grandpa and sing and dance. I miss him so much.

I like musicals way more than the symphony. Dad won't let us say anything or even get up during the symphony orchestra in the park concerts. We sit real quiet on our blankets, so he can hear the music he loves. We usually fall asleep half-way through the performances.

When Mom lays out the picnic treats, we take a break from singing and dancing to eat ham-and-cheese sandwiches. After dinner, we lie down on our picnic blankets and watch the show until it's dark out, then we head home. As we approach the house, we stop to gaze at the twinkling stars in the night sky. Fireflies flash their tiny lights all around us. It's magical. I say to myself, *Star light, star bright, first star I see tonight. Wish I may. Wish I might. Get the wish, I wish tonight. I wish we were back in the East Coast with our relatives.* Tonight was the last night of the outdoor concerts. Summer is ending, and winter is around the corner.

* * *

Months have passed and it's our first winter in Cincinnati. I love the winter, as it reminds me of Connecticut. I didn't like living in Los Angeles, because it didn't snow there. It's Sunday and we get up early to go to church with Mom. Dad doesn't go to church with us, thank God. He says all the church wants is our money.

After church, Paul, Meagan, and I ride our bikes to a nearby lake, where we go ice skating. I love riding my bike really fast down the steep hills. The cold wind blows into my face and through my hair. I extend my arms like a bird, steer my bike with balance, and flap my wings. I don't have a care in the world. Paul beats me to the lake, as always. I don't mind, though. I go a little slower to prevent crashing. Plus, there is sand on the road from the snow a few days earlier.

We learned to skate in Connecticut. Mom bought skates for the older kids and I got their hand-me-downs. This time, I didn't mind because they were snugly worn after my older sisters broke them in for me. I absolutely love skating with the kids in the neighborhood. We often play tag on skates. When I'm "it," I see my little sister struggling on her skates, I skate over to her, touch her shoulder, and say, "Tag! You're it!" She smirks and grumbles something under her breath. I smile and skate away. Skating comes easily to me; I'm a skilled and confident skater.

No matter the season, I like to be outside playing with our friends in the neighborhood. In the summertime, we play Capture the Flag and Kick the Can in our yards. My grandpa was right about a stranger being a friend you haven't met yet. We have a lot more friends here.

It's too cold to be outside, so Paul, Meagan, and I are inside playing cards around the kitchen table while our dad is in the living room listening to his classical music. Yuck! Debbie is at her girlfriend's house. She can drive now, so she borrowed the car. I wish I was old enough to drive. Mom is talking on the phone to our older siblings in the kitchen. I miss them and wonder what they are doing.

When Daniel got back from Vietnam, he found a job in Los Angeles at TRW, a company that makes satellites. I don't know what a satellite is, but he is making good money. He bought a house, so Patty moved in with him. I wish I could stay with them. I can tell Mom misses them because she calls them a lot. Dad doesn't like her to call them so much, as it's expensive to call long distance. Laura is living near them, too. She got married to the guy Patty used to date.

When Mom hangs up, I ask, "What were you talking about?"

She says, "We are moving to San Diego, California. Your father got a job in Chula Vista, which is in San Diego! It's just two hours away from Daniel and your sisters!"

We jump up and down and scream; we are elated to be moving closer to our brother and sisters.

Dads yells from the living room, "Stop screaming! I can't hear my music!"

We skitter to our rooms. I wonder if he got fired from this job, too. He doesn't seem to be getting better. In fact, he seems to be getting worse. Mom has been asking him to find a job in California, and I am glad he finally did. Maybe he didn't get fired. Who knows? I will miss the friends I've made over the past two years, but I am glad we are moving to be near my brother and sisters.

Luckily, Dad is driving out to California alone in another sports car he bought. We will drive there in the station wagon in a few days after we pack up the house. A moving company will take everything to San Diego. Mom is driving us there with Debbie's help.

After a long day of driving, we found a motel with two queen beds in Tulsa, Oklahoma. Debbie shares a bed with Mom, and Paul, Meagan and I are in the other bed. The last night we stop in Flagstaff, Arizona and get a room with two beds in it again. I'm so happy I don't have to sleep on the hard floor. We have more fun on this trip driving to California. We are silly, laughing and singing the whole way there. No one yells at us and ruins our fun.

> ***Watching my life being played out in front of me, I remember feeling good about leaving my old friends behind in California. I never felt the same after Mr. Wilson took advantage of me. I felt like an outcast.***

Chapter Five

Twelve Going on Fourteen

I don't have to go to Catholic School in San Diego, because it costs too much. I'm relieved; I didn't like it anyway. I am in sixth grade at public school. I can wear whatever I want, and I don't have to go to church every day, either. We go on field trips, and Mom volunteers to help drive me and my classmates in our big car. On this trip, we are at the planetarium. I have never been to one before. It's cool, looking through a big telescope and seeing the different planets.

I miss my old friends in Ohio, but I am making new ones in San Diego. Grandpa was right, strangers are friends you haven't met yet. I like making new friends.

I love the time after school before Dad storms in and wrecks everything. We can be as goofy and as loud as we want without someone telling us to shut up. Mom often plays the piano while I act out the songs. I know all the songs from *Fiddler on the Roof* and *The Sound of Music* by heart. I love being the performer in our family. I took piano lessons for a while when I was younger, but I didn't like it, so I quit. I like listening to my mom play, though. She is teaching me all kinds of songs to act out, like "Mamma's Little Baby Likes Shortening Bread." I am having so much fun. One day I am going to be a Broadway or Hollywood star. I think I fit the part with my long blonde hair, big green eyes, and slender figure. I ditched the cat-eyed glasses and now have wire pilot frames. Mom wanted to be a movie star when she was younger. She could have been; she is stunningly beautiful.

My mom isn't the only talented piano player in our family. Paul is also great, especially when he plays the boogie-woogie. When he's at the piano, I soak in the music and think about how much I look up to him. Like me, Meagan struggles to play the piano, so she acts out the songs with me. I am always the star of our skits, though.

* * *

There are only four kids living at home. Debbie is 19 and the oldest sibling at home, so she takes care of us. I'm surprised she hasn't married David, her boyfriend who lives next door. He is cute and charming, just like Debbie. She has silky, long brown hair, a beautiful smile, and is sweet like Mom. She and David sing beautiful duets at church and Bible study. When they sing together, and he plays the guitar, they are like two lovebirds. I can see why Debbie loves him. I'm am sure they will marry one day. I, too, want to marry my Prince Charming and be whisked away on a white horse. A girl can dream; can't she?

* * *

It's my birthday, April 18, 1974, but it's not special like most birthdays. In fact, it's the worst possible birthday. We found out that Mom has ovarian cancer. She'd been in a lot of pain down there, so she got checked out by a doctor. After a bunch of tests, during which the whole family was on pins and needles waiting for the results, the doctor delivered the bad news, gave her pain medication, and said there was nothing more he could do for her.

I don't know what that means. Shouldn't a doctor be able to help her? I heard Deborah talking to our older siblings on the phone, saying, "She's in God's capable hands now."

Please God, take care of our mother! Do you hear me?

* * *

Today is a special day — July 7, 1974, my mom's birthday. Our Grandfather and Aunt Florence, my mom's favorite sister, are here from Rhode Island to celebrate. My dad is at work, thank God. I can't remember the last time I was this happy. Hearing Grandpa play the banjo while Mom is playing the piano is music to my ears. She loves the songs from *Jesus Christ Super Star*. She's playing, "I Don't Know How to Love Him," the song that Mary Magdalene sings to Jesus. My mom's name is Mary, too. I think she loves it because it reminds her of how much she loves the Lord. I know God will heal Mom. He can't take her away from us. I would miss her so much and can't imagine life without her.

I say this prayer: *Please, Lord, spare our mother. You can take Dad if you want. No one would miss him, except Mom. And maybe not even her.*

We made carrot cake cupcakes with cream cheese frosting — Mom's favorite. Deborah helps her blow out the candle. I make a wish. It is no surprise what my wish is.

But Mom isn't hungry. She barely takes a bite. So, I eat two cupcakes — one for me and one for her. I feel stuffed, but it's for a good cause.

With mom being sick, I wish I knew my older siblings better. Laurie is 22 years old, married, and lives about an hour away. She is an accomplished classical piano player. She probably learned to play classical music for Dad. But even Laurie's playing isn't enough. Nothing anyone seems to do is good enough for Dad.

Daniel still lives in Long Beach and still works at TRW. I thank the Lord for bringing him back to us. Some of his buddies didn't make it.

Today, Patty, who was in charge of me growing up, is visiting us. I hear her say to Mom that she doesn't like Los Angeles, because she doesn't like to come home from work to see her roommates and their friends lying around partying. But it's 1974 and everyone parties. I wish I was old enough to party. I'm 12 now. Before Daniel went to Vietnam, I used to love watching my older siblings partying with their friends.

* * *

It's late November, and Debbie tends to Mom, whose cancer has spread throughout her body, leaving her bedridden. Debbie made her Campbell's Chicken Noodle Soup, which I love, but Mom didn't touch it. Later, I see the bowl of soup sitting on the kitchen counter, so I reheat it in an empty saucepan on the stove. I can tell Mom is in immense pain. She doesn't say much and sleeps a lot. She was always curvy, but now she is super thin, frail, and always tired. It's so quiet in the house. No one plays the piano or sings anymore, because we don't want to disturb her. Where's God? I'm afraid he isn't listening to our prayers to heal Mom.

Debbie urges Dad to take Mom to the hospital. I pray the doctors there can help her. I don't like to see her in such pain. She hasn't played the piano since Grandpa was here for her birthday. I feel so empty inside. Debbie is doing her best to take care of us, but it's not the same without Mom. I feel like I'm holding my breath until Mom comes home for good. I spend a lot of time on the lower bunk in my bedroom staring at the empty upper bunk. At least we all have our own rooms now.

It's Thanksgiving Day and Debbie tells us that Mom can come home today for dinner. She has been in the hospital for a few weeks. I am so excited! What an incredible day it will be! I am so thankful to God for hearing our prayers and healing Mom.

Meagan and I set the dining room table with our good Currier and Ives china we received when my dad's mother died. It's creamy white porcelain and has scenes of the French countryside painted in cobalt blue. Debbie and Paul are making dinner.

Dad goes to the hospital to get Mom. We were expecting them by 1:00, but it's 2:15 and they aren't home yet. I wonder what is taking so long. The side dishes are getting cold. I can't wait to see Mom and celebrate Thanksgiving with her. We make the final preparations by taking the turkey out of the oven. Debbie gently slides the homemade pumpkin and pecan pies into the oven, so they are warm when we are ready to eat them after dinner. The turkey looks so moist and juicy. She takes the drippings from the pan to make Mom's homemade gravy recipe. I love smashed potatoes with her homemade gravy. We call them smashed potatoes, because we don't like them creamy. We smash the potatoes but leave lots of lumps and add butter and tarragon. The scent of pies fills the air. It smells like the cinnamon and raisin bread Grandma toasted for us when we were kids — like heaven on earth. I miss Grandma and Grandpa. I wish they were here with us. But I thank the Lord for hearing our prayers and bringing Mom home.

When the phone rings at three o'clock, Debbie answers it. Dad tells her to go ahead and eat without them. We sit down to Thanksgiving dinner, but no one is hungry. We push the cold food around on our plates in silence.

Debbie says, "Mom probably can't eat much, anyway. It's better that we get ready for her after dinner. How about if we do a little performance?"

I perk up. "I am going to do 'Momma's Little Baby Likes Shortening Bread.'" She loves that song.

I run into my room to put on my costume — a big white cotton dress with blue flowers, the kind Grandma wears. I bought this dress at the Salvation Army, one of our favorite stores. I stuff a pillow in it to make me look fat. Then I head to the bathroom to put grease paint on my face. I had some left over from when I was learning to mime. I paint my face black and my lips white. I can't wait to be the star of the show! I tie a red bandana around my head and tuck my hair in. I check out my costume; I look like a big black lady. My heart is beating out of my chest! I can't wait to raise my mom's spirits.

There's a knock at the door and my dad comes in. He looks awful.

"I need you to be a soldier," Dad says.

"No, I am going to be Momma, in Momma's Little Babies Like Shortening Bread," I say.

I can see he is as confused as me.

"Mom is in heaven having a cup of tea with Jesus," he says.

Huh? Mom loves tea, but how can she be having tea with Jesus? Is Jesus here? I am going to perform for Mom right now.

I leave the bathroom and walk into the living room where everyone is crying. I look around for Mom. Why didn't she come home? Debbie is speaking to me, but I can't understand her. This just can't be. God promised me a miracle today. We went to prayer meetings to pray for Mom's healing. But we knew it would come; it was a matter of time. I can feel my heart breaking into a million pieces. I vow to never love anyone again. It hurts too much. I return to the bathroom, take my costume off, and wash the grease paint off my face. My tears are frozen. My stomach is in knots. I grab onto the bathroom vanity as I feel like I'm going to faint. I look at my face in the mirror and see mom's face looking back at me.

Why didn't you say good-bye?

* * *

A few days later, Deborah is cleaning out Mom's dresser and finds a letter dated September 30, 1974. She is reading it aloud while recording it on a cassette player to send to my grandfather. I'm sitting next to her while she's talking into the microphone of the cassette player. I'm hearing mom's words, but I don't understand them. Maybe one day I will.

I might have known it would take a biggie to get me to set a few things down in black and white. And we might say cancer is a biggie. Oddly enough, I call it a gift because it gives me an opportunity to discover how I would react to it. We all have often wondered, what if? Strange to say, regarding this thing, I never have. Guess I thought I was indestructible. Besides I didn't smoke, drink, or even eat much, or do anything associated with shortening one's life. Yet, here it is. It's happened. So, what to do? Nothing really, except take the prescribed treatment and hope for the best. And what is the best? Ah, that's the question. In my case, I have it made either way. If I stay, I'm surrounded by more loving family and friends than most monarchs can claim. And if I go, well, isn't that what we were destined for since the beginning of time?

To think that I have been in the mind of God and therefore part of His plan since before the beginning is awesome indeed. And if He chooses that my moment in history is over and we are meant to meet, who am I to argue? No one, nor anything, has held me completely, except God. Part of me has held back a little from the ones I love and the things I enjoy. I've deliberately never completely wrapped myself up in anyone or anything. Perhaps our transient existence precludes this. It's a defense mechanism against loss and grief. And so, I turned to the constant, my ever-present, never-changing God. He , and He only, knows the many me's. He knows the me I was meant to be and wearily I've shined to reach that ideal me-ness. Why are we so possessed with being what we are not? The best compliment we can pay our Maker is to be ourselves.

I look at life as walking along two parallels. One measures our attitudes towards God, others and ourselves and is the basis for our own individual appraisal. But, the other records our stakes on the whole picture. We must pay for our time here by leaving something of value behind. And what can most of us leave? For myself, I'm sort of an un-person — unscientific, unmechanical, untalented and the list goes on.

So, not having any real gifts, I become a steppingstone to discovery. We can't all be the pathfinders. Some of us must be the path. That means being trampled on. And if this life were all there was, it surely wouldn't be fair. But this isn't life at all, it's only the front porch and only Death will open the door.

* * *

We are at mom's funeral at Saint Pius the Tenth. The church is packed. The scent of burning incense permeates the air. Normally I don't mind the smell, but today I feel like I might puke. We sit in the front row, looking or trying not to look, at our mother in an open casket. I can't believe the person in the coffin is my mom.

She had long beautiful gray hair and was always smiling. They butchered her hair and gave her awful corkscrew curls, or is it a wig? And she's frowning. That can't be my mom. I simply can't go up there to see her. I am empty and cannot cry, even though a flood of tears pools in my heart. I remain in the pew, holding on for dear life, while my brothers, sisters, and father go see her. Everyone is wearing long faces saying how sorry they are. Sometimes I can't even make out what they're saying. It's as if I suddenly lost the ability to understand my own language.

We drive to Holy Cross Cemetery to bury our mother. I sit in the back of the car with Paul, and Meagan. I am looking but I don't see; I am listening, but I don't hear; I am sensing but I don't feel. Dad is driving and Debbie is sitting in Mom's seat. How dare anyone sit in her seat? That seat is reserved for Mom, even if she is gone. I haven't said a word since the dreadful day she died.

Out the back window, the neighborhoods look rough with graffiti everywhere, like there must be lots of gang activity. The homes are dilapidated and trash litters the streets. It's a cold, late November day, overcast with black clouds looming over us.

Watching her casket lower into the ground, I feel as if I am being buried with her, not a piece of me, but all of me. I'm freezing and shaking, and my teeth are chattering. I want to go home, not that there's any comfort there anymore. It looks like it's going to rain. I hear thunder in the distance. The last words out of the priest's mouth are, "May Mary rest in peace." How can he say that? This isn't happening! A loving God would not take our mother and leave us with our father. I feel betrayed. *I hate you, God! Do you hear me? I feel betrayed. I will never trust you again.*

> ***Looking down from this heavenly perspective, I realize now our mother was the glue that held our family together, and, without her, much worse was yet to come. If I had known then, what was in store for me, I may have taken my own life. I am glad I didn't, but what is God trying to teach me? What lessons do I need to learn? What do I need to let go?***

Chapter Six

Fourteen Going on Sixteen

I haven't said a word in six months. When I go to school, I can hear Mrs. Jones, our teacher, talking, but I am not listening.

The office secretary walks into class with a new girl, whispers something to Mrs. Jones, and then leaves.

Mrs. Jones says, "Class, I want to introduce Nancy Sawyer. She just moved here from Texas."

Nancy smiles and says, "Hi, yawl," with a deep Southern accent. She sits down in the front of the class — the only empty seat. I'm in the back row by the window, daydreaming about what it would be like if Mom were still here.

My old friends have abandoned me, just like my Mom. Perhaps they don't know what to say to someone who has completely checked out. I tried to talk after Mom died, but I didn't know what to say, so I didn't say anything. It doesn't matter. I don't need them anyway. They don't understand how it feels to have your whole world come crashing down around you. I wish someone would get what I am going through. I want someone to talk to; I just don't know how to begin. My breath is shallow, making it hard to breathe. Will I ever be the old Jackie or is she gone forever?

I walk home through the soccer fields behind my school and then take a shortcut through Telegraph Canyon. I like it, as hardly anyone goes this way. Most kids walk on the streets, which is much longer, or they take the bus. The new girl walks up beside me and smiles. She takes a toke off a joint. She holds the smoke in as long as she can and then blows it out with a deep sigh. Her grin is so big, she looks like the Cheshire cat. She hands me the joint. I don't want her to think I am uncool, so I take a hit, even though I've never tried it before. I mimic my father, who smokes cigarettes, and my older brother and sisters, who smoked pot in front of me when I was a kid. The smoke burns my lungs. I can't hold it for long, like she did. I start coughing. She is laughing at me. I am laughing, too. It feels so good to finally laugh.

"What's your name?" she asks.

"Jackie."

"My name is Nan. I noticed you in class. I just moved here from Abilene, Texas."

I look at her with sad eyes and say, "Welcome. I hope you like it here," as sincerely as I can. Nan is the only person I've spoken to in months. It's nice to hear my own voice again.

She is so pretty. She has a curvy body with long blonde hair like mine. I am sure the guys at school think she's sexy. She's funny, too. I wish I had a figure like hers. I am skinny. I don't eat much.

We walk to her house, which is not far from mine. It's a rental home resembling ours, but in disrepair. The place is bare. A few pieces of furniture and some unopened boxes are scattered about.

"Welcome to my humble abode," Nan snickers. "We left in a hurry and didn't have time to take our stuff." She claims she's going to get new stuff.

No one is home, so Nan lights up another joint. She takes a long drag, then passes the joint and says, "We moved here last week. My mom was transferred here by her company. She and my dad divorced a long time ago. I'm an only child. Lucky me."

"You *are* lucky. I feel like I get lost in the crowd with my siblings," I say. Glancing at the clock I realize it's almost dinnertime. "I should go home. My sister Debbie is probably wondering where I am."

"I'll walk you home. I want to see where you live," Nan says.

My house is one street over on Monserate Avenue, the second from the corner on the opposite side of the street. I pause at the corner before we cross the street and stop in front of my house. "Do you want to come in?"

"No, that's okay. I'll see you tomorrow at school," she says.

Debbie is cooking dinner, so I sneak into my bedroom. I don't want to run into anyone because they'll know I'm high. It's a little scary — like going down a steep rollercoaster. I have butterflies in my stomach. It feels kinda good, though.

Dad's car pulls up and he walks down the breezeway toward the front door. Dad and Debbie talk in the kitchen for a few minutes, then Debbie calls us in for dinner. Paul and Meagan emerge from their rooms and head into the kitchen. I am glad that we have our own rooms, so I can have my own space. I head to the bathroom to brush my teeth and freshen up.

I am the last to sit down at the kitchen table . I am still a little high, but I don't mind. It feels good to feel something for a change. The pungent aroma of chicken and rice only makes me hungrier. We all dive into our dinners.

I look at my Dad and say, "Pass the salt, please."

He looks startled and amazed. He can't believe I'm talking. No one has heard me say anything for so long. They all start talking to me.

"How was your day at school, Jackie?" Debbie says.

"Good! I met a new girl from Texas."

She says, "That's great!" in her positive, enthusiastic way, like Mom.

It feels good to talk again. I can tell everyone is happy, including me. At least I think I am. I haven't been happy for so long, I forgot what it feels like. After dinner, I go to my room and clean it from top to bottom. I don't know where I am getting all this energy, but I am not complaining.

I have Mom's entire collection of *Reader's Digest* short stories. I understand why Mom always read them. They are good. I fall asleep reading a short story from one of her *Reader's Digests* called, "Mrs. Starr Lives Alone." It's creepy.

I wake up with the sunrise, as usual. The early bird gets the worm, right? I am excited because it's Friday. I love Fridays because it means two days without school. I hate school because of the cliques and the fact that most kids think they are better than I am. At least that's how it feels. It's nice to finally meet someone more like me. I take a shower and head to Nan's so we can walk to school together.

"Do you want to spend the night tonight?" I ask.

She smiles at me with her warm charm. "That would be awesome!"

Nan and I are both in Mrs. Jones' American history class. We are learning about the Great Depression. I feel checked-in for the first time in forever. It's fascinating thinking about my mom at my age enduring the Depression. I think I have it bad but having no money would have been worse.

After class Nan says, "I met a cute guy in my math class who invited me to meet him at the park after school. Want to go with me?"

"Sure! Let's go!"

We run across the street to Hilltop, a big city park with the same name as our school. Scanning the park, I see moms watching their kids playing on a swing set and guys sitting at a picnic table underneath a gazebo.

Nan teases me. "It looks like he brought a friend for you."

I am a little nervous but act cool. I will follow her lead.

We sit down with them. Nan says, "Clint, isn't it?" smiling at a big gorgeous, tanned guy with long straight blond hair.

He says, "This is my friend, Billy," and glances at his friend sitting next to him.

"This is my friend, Jackie." She smiles at me real big.

I say, "Hi," and smile, too.

Nan is extremely sociable. The guys are fun to hang out with. I like that they are asking lots of questions about us. Billy has long, straight brown hair pulled into a ponytail.

He looks at me and says, "I've seen you around school."

"Yeah, I've seen you, too. Nan just moved here from Texas."

Clint says to Nan, "Are you a cowgirl? Did you ride horses there?"

She giggles and says, "As a matter of fact, I did. My uncle has a ranch."

Nan pulls out a joint from her cigarette pack and says to Clint, "Want to smoke a joint?"

He says, "Hell, yeah! Light it up!"

We smoke together under the covered picnic table. We talk for a while about their favorite hangouts. They mention they are going to the J Street Marina parking lot this weekend with some friends who race cars. They asked us to join them on Saturday night.

Nan says, "Sounds like fun! Maybe we'll see you there."

Nan and I walk over to her house to grab some things before we head to my house.

"I think Clint and Billy are so cute. Don't you?" She nudges my arm with her elbow.

"They are total foxes!" I say, with a shit-eating grin. She laughs.

I love her laugh. It's contagious. I can't remember the last time I laughed this much.

She grabs a duffle bag and throws some clothes and toiletries into it. She hands me a boombox and a case of cassette tapes. She walks out of her room into the kitchen and writes a note and leaves it on the table for her mom. We head to my house.

We are hanging out in my room. It used to be Debbie's room before she moved across the hall. I put the bunk beds that my little sister and I had in our old room, side by side in the middle of the room. With my Dad's help, Debbie hung burlap on the walls with wallpaper paste and nailed stained boards on the walls vertically to hide the seams from the burlap. She's extremely artistic and can paint and draw, too. I wish I could draw as well as my sister. My contribution is taking pictures of horses from magazines and tacking them up on the burlap walls. On one side of the room there is a window that opens to a dog run and on the other wall, a window next to the front door. I often gaze out the window and dream of having a dog. I've asked for a dog several times over the years. My Mom always gave me the same answer: "We have enough mouths to feed. We don't need any more."

Nan and I listen to some great cassette tapes on her boombox, including Pink Floyd's "Dark Side of the Moon" and Led Zeppelin's "Stairway to Heaven."

I say, "I love the words to 'Stairway to Heaven.' 'There's a lady who's sure all that glitters are gold, and she's buying a stairway to heaven.' I wish I could buy a stairway to heaven. I'm sure my Mom is there."

Nan says, "What happened to your mom?"

I shudder. "She died of cancer last Thanksgiving."

She puts her arm around me. "I'm sorry. Do you want to smoke?"

I am a little nervous, but I don't want her to think I am afraid. "Sure, but let's blow it out the window."

I love hanging out with her. She has a real sweet personality and cracks me up. We fall asleep around

10:00 p.m. listening to our music and swapping stories of our lives.

Around 11:15, I hear Debbie and Paul returning from the Friday night prayer meeting. I used to go with them to pray for a miracle when Mom was dying. God didn't deliver, so I don't go anymore. Fuck God! They are banging loudly on the door; they must have forgotten their keys. My dad yells at them as he walks down the hall to unlock the front door.

Nan wakes up to my father and sister shouting. I turn toward her and put my index finger to my lips, "Shhh!" so she'll be quiet.

Dad shouts, "Where the fuck have you been and why are you coming home this late?"

"We went to the prayer meeting at church and hung out for a little while. Sorry, we didn't bring a key. I thought the door would be unlocked," Debbie says meekly.

Dad screams, "Why go to those damned prayer meetings? Your fucking God took your mother away!" He pushes Debbie while saying it and she falls at his feel, flat on the ground.

I glance at Nan and back out the window. Debbie is lying on the ground staring up at my dad. He begins swinging an axe over her head like a madman. I gasp and cover my mouth. He won't kill her. Will he? She's pressing her head into the ground. If she raises it, the axe will hit her in the face. The fear in her eyes is terrifying. I hope Dad can't see me. I want to duck, but I can't move away from the horror of it all.

Paul sprints to the neighbor's house. A few minutes later, a siren screams down the street. He must have called the police. Dad puts down the axe and heads into the house. Debbie gets up and runs next door to her boyfriend's house. A police car pulls up, lights flashing, lighting up our house. I'm relieved that my little sister spent the night at her friend's house.

We can barely hear the conversation going on in the living room. The police are talking to my dad when my sister and brother walk into the house. The cops question my sister. I'm trying hard to hear what they are saying. When I hear shuffling and the front door closing, I look out the window to see my dad handcuffed in his underwear. He is holding a bag, which I assume contains his clothes. They shove him into the back of the police car.

The neighbors are gathered outside watching the cop car drive away. I am so humiliated. I want to punch a wall, but I don't because Nan is with me. I can't even have a friend in my life without my father ruining it for me. I always knew he was crazy, but this is taking it to a whole new level. I wonder what Mom would think.

I look at Nan and say, "He's a madman! How could he do this to us? That fucker!"

"I guess I won't complain anymore about not having a dad in my life." Nan looks right at me and says, "Who needs 'em?"

I really like Nan. She gets me. At least there is one person in the universe who sees what I go through and still wants to be my friend. We hear my sister and brother go into their bedrooms.

Nan says, "Your dad is crazy."

"Yeah, no kidding. I hope they throw away the key and he never comes back."

She laughs, sits up, rolls a joint, and lights up. I sit up in my bed and she passes it to me. I walk over to the window, slide it open, then blow my smoke outside.

"It smells like a Christmas tree in here. I hope they can't smell it," I say softly.

She giggles. We are whispering, as I don't want my sister to come in. I walk back to my bed and lie down. I close my eyes and can feel the room rocking from side to side, like I am in my mother's arms. Oh, how I wish she were here. I fall asleep dreaming of her.

I wake up early after a restless night without sleep. I am hungry, so I head to the kitchen to get some cereal for Nan and me. Paul is at the table eating breakfast.

"Where's Debbie?" I ask.

"She went to the police station for more questioning," says Paul.

Nan is still sleeping, so I eat breakfast with my brother. I am glad he is here. He has always been my rock, my ground-wire, so to speak.

"I am glad you called the police last night. I hope he stays in jail and rots," I say.

"How did you know I called the police?"

I say with a sly expression, "I saw everything out my window. If the cops need a witness, I can tell them exactly what happened last night. I'm just glad you guys are okay. What was he thinking, swinging that axe around? I think he has seriously lost it."

A few minute later, my sister walks into the house with my dad. We shut up. I rush back to my room and find Nan awake.

"Shit! He's back! I guess Debbie didn't press charges." I hand her a bowl of cereal.

She says, "Thanks, but I'm not hungry. Let's get out of here."

"Follow me," I say.

We jump out my window. It feels good to be out in the cool, crisp morning air. I can finally breathe.

"Why don't you spend the night at my house?" Nan asks.

"That would be great!"

"You can borrow my clothes. I think we're about the same size."

We see Paul walking our way. "Hey, where are you going?" he says.

"I'm spending the weekend at Nan's."

He looks at her and says, "Hi," with a serious face. He glances at me and says, "Debbie said that Dad told the police he thought someone was breaking in, so that's why he had an axe."

"Yeah, but once he saw it was you two, why did he continue to wave the axe around?

I can't believe she didn't press charges. How could she do that to us?"

He shrugs his shoulders and glances down with a frown.

I hate my life. I am so ashamed Nan witnessed this.

"I feel for you, girl. You can stay with me as long as you want," says Nan.

"I'll be at Nan's, if anyone asks," I say to Paul.

He nods and heads back into the nuthouse. I wish we could all escape.

I stay with Nan until after school on Monday. No one even asks me where I've been.

On Monday night, I am lying on my bed remembering a story my older brother and sisters told us kids about something that happened to them before we were born. Sadly, the axe incident wasn't our first horror story.

Mom was at the grocery store and my older siblings were playing in the basement. They must have gotten out of control, yelling and screaming. Dad came down with a gun and ordered them to line up against a wall. He told them not to move or he would blow them away. They just stood there until Mom came home a few minutes later. When she hollered downstairs that she was home, my dad quickly hid the gun and went upstairs. No one ever told her. They were afraid of what Dad would do to them or, worse yet, what he would do to Mom.

She always got the brunt of his wrath while we hid in our rooms. She would just sit there while he screamed at her and he threw things on the ground. It's scary when Dad flies into fits of rage. He has never hit anyone; he just uses emotional warfare to scare the shit out of us. Now we are all alone without her to protect us. *I can't believe God took her and left us with this madman. What kind of God would do that? I hate my dad and wish he would die.*

* * *

Meanwhile, Dad signs up with an organization called We Care, where widows, widowers, and divorcees go to meet people. Last weekend he went bowling and didn't take us.

One Saturday only a few weeks after the incident with the police, he says we're going to a dance at Balboa Park. We don't want to go, but we don't want him to get mad, so Meagan, Paul, and I agree to go.

The polka band that's playing reminds me of my Grandpa's music. Dad met a divorcee named Lucille. Evidently, he's seen her a few other times before tonight.

Dad says, "Kids, Dad and Lucille are getting married. She is going to be your new stepmom."

Say what? It has only been six months since mom died.

Paul, Meagan, and I just look at each other with blank stares. "We're happy for you," I say with a smirk.

They got married at a Justice of the Peace. I don't know what that is, and I don't really care. Lucille can have him. I can't believe he married her just six months after Mom died. I hate her. She's nothing like my mom. She has short red hair and constantly wears a frown. She's fat and binges on junk food. She doesn't prepare home-cooked meals like Mom, either. Everything she cooks comes out of a can and tastes like aluminum. She just lies around watching soap operas while we are at school. Little does she know that her life is about to become one big soap opera. I think Dad just wants someone to take care of us kids. The problem is, he hasn't told her. The only way I will survive is to stop feeling anything at all.

* * *

It's been less than a year since mom died and Debbie marries the guy next door. It was just a matter of time. It isn't a big wedding, just a few friends and family at the church. I guess she figures we are taken care of now, so she can get on with her life. I wish I could get married and get the hell out of here. There are only three of us kids left at home — Paul, Meagan, and me. We don't hang out much anymore; ever since Mom died, we just hide in our rooms.

I hang out with the kids at school called Loadies; we're given that name because we like to get loaded. There are also Soc's who are very social, and Jocks who are athletes, but I am definitely a Loady. We live 15 miles from the Mexican border, so pot and other good drugs are plentiful.

Tonight, we are at a guy's house who gave everyone a hit of acid. I've never taken acid before and it's making me feel real paranoid. We are hanging out in the front yard. A gang of Mexicans are walking down the street towards us. The problem with living so close to the border is that there are lots of Mexican gangs.

A guy in our group says, "Fuckin' Beaners" as they pass.

A Chicano pulls out his switchblade and says, "What did you say?"

I am so afraid, I jump over the fence and run home. It's called survival of the fittest. My mamma didn't raise no fool.

Nan is cleaning a drug dealer's house in exchange for drugs. She invites me to go with her today. He is at least 10 or 15 years older than we are. He is unattractive and heavy set with a beer belly but acts like a real ladies' man. It's obvious he drinks a lot of beer. Who else would have a beer tap on their refrigerator? He pours us a frothy beer and takes Tupperware containers out of a cabinet filled with colorful pills. Nan tells me they are called Rainbows, Reds, and Yellow Jackets, and she explains what each one does to you. It's like a 31-Flavors ice cream parlor for pills. He opens a container filled with Reds and offers me some. I've never taken pills before, so I'm a little apprehensive. I've tried acid, but it's not a pill; it's a tiny piece of paper.

I won't do that again. I like pot, as I am still in control. I hate feeling out of control, like when I'm at home.

Nan says the Reds make her too relaxed, so she takes a Yellow Jacket, which she says gives her energy. I take a Red to relax. I am always stressing and obsessing about my life — usually about my dad or stepmom. Mixing drugs with a few beers is making me feel tired and dizzy. I don't know where the drug dealer went. I lie down to get some sleep while Nan finishes cleaning. When I wake up in a strange bed, I feel groggy and disoriented. *Where am I? Where's Nan? Did I fall asleep while she was cleaning?*

As I come to, I notice my pants are off and there is blood on the sheets. I don't remember getting undressed before falling asleep. It hurts like hell down there, too. *Did he fuck me? I can't believe he did that.* I have never had sex before, but I know what it is. The guy is in the shower. I notice my clothes are in a heap on the floor. I dress quickly. Nan is nowhere to be found. I duck out the front door before that prick gets out of the shower. I will never take pills again! I can't believe he did that. That fucker! I hate men. In the past, when I heard the song, "It Feels Like the First Time," by Foreigner, I would daydream about falling in love for the first time. Now I feel like I can't trust men anymore. Another dream shattered.

On my way home, I see the neighbor lady in her front yard watering her roses. She asks me if I can babysit tonight. I could use the money, so I agree to watch her kids.

Her kids are cool. They just want to watch movies. I make popcorn with tons of butter and salt. Their cockapoo — a cocker spaniel and poodle mix — had puppies and they're crawling all over us. I am in puppy heaven. I sure wish I could have a dog. I am cuddling with one on the couch next to the kids, and they are holding the other two. We fall asleep after watching a movie. When their parent's come home, she takes the puppy out of my arms, I wake up.

The neighbor lady says, "You should take one of the puppies."

"I doubt my dad will let me, but I'll ask him and let you know."

She gives me five bucks. I say, "Thanks!" I could get used to this. I walk across the street to my house and go to bed. I am exhausted. No one ever asks me where I'm going or when I am coming home. It's like no one really cares.

The next day, my dad is working on the car in the driveway. I try to get up the nerve to ask him if I can have a puppy. I know he will say no, but I really want one, so I ask anyway.

He takes his wallet out his back pocket and says, "Sure, how much are they?"

I am so excited that I give him a big hug. I can't remember the last time we hugged. "They're free! I promise I'll take good care of it."

I run across the street to tell the neighbor lady. She smiles and invites me in to pick one out. There are three puppies left from a litter of six, including one that looks like the runt. He is smaller than the others and gets picked on by the bigger ones.

I say, "I'd like this one." I think she's happy I took the runt. I scoop him up and head home. He reminds me of myself, the underdog.

Dad looks happy when he sees me carrying our new puppy. He always had dogs growing up. He promises to show me how to train him. I couldn't be happier. The fact that he is willing to pay for him without any argument encourages me that he will follow through on his promise. The puppy is so cute with dark brown curly hair and dark brown eyes that look like chocolate drops. We name him Jacob, after a dog his father gave him. My dad and I teach him all kinds of tricks; he can give me five and ten, lie down, roll over, and play dead. Jacob and I become best friends and go everywhere together.

Dad is going sailing after work today. He likes to go on weekdays, as it's too busy on the weekends. He keeps his sailboat at the J Street Marina near our house.

* * *

Nan and I often hang out at J Street Marina on Saturday nights with our friends who own hot-rod cars. We bring booze from our parents' stashes tonight. A guy name Dick asks me if I want to drive his 1949 Anglia with nitrous injection later.

I say, "Hell, yeah! Let the good times roll."

Dick is cute, but much older than I am. He is tall and tan with blond curly hair that looks like an afro. He's like a big-brother figure to me. I like hanging out with him. He always beats the other guys. I think that's why he calls the shots around here. He tells the others, "Jackie will start the race for us."

I smile at Dick, walk over to the starting line, and make eye contact with each of the guys lined up ready to race. One guy has a midnight blue 1967 Chevelle Super Sport and the other guy is driving a red 1969 Ford

Mustang fastback. I extend my arms. When I drop them, the guys take off and race each other, two at a time. It's so great!

It is amazing listening to their engines rev up and take off. Dick could have any girl here and he picks me. I can tell he likes me. I really dig him, too. He's showing me how to drive his hot rod now that the races are over. Its fun driving the Anglia. Nan gives me a big smile and a wink. I smile back and laugh. She's so funny.

I never asked her where she was the day I got raped, nor did I tell her what happened. It's weird how I can remember the color of the underwear I had on, but I can't remember anything that he did to me. I just want to forget it ever happened.

The guys at school have tried to get close to me, but they are so immature. I feel so much older than I am. Dick is 24, 10 years older than I am. Plus, he has a few cars, so it's much easier to get around when I'm his co-pilot. He has tried to have sex with me, but I told him I want to wait. He is a little shy, so he hasn't pushed the issue.

* * *

Dad asks us kids if we want to go to the beach later while he is sailing.

We all say, "Yeah!"

We put beach towels and bathing suits in our backpacks so he can pick us up after school. I can't wait!

I say, "Bring Jacob with you!"

That's the one thing my Dad and I have in common — Jacob. He takes him everywhere! We both really love him. I think my dad might love him more than he loves us.

Dad drops us off at the beach and drives to the marina.

"Jacob and I are going swimming," I shout. It's a scorching hot day. The sun is shining brightly on the horizon. It's so peaceful; the beach is practically empty. Cute little sandpipers skitter down the beach, chirping as they go. There's a nice steady breeze, so I know Dad will be happy. We swim while Dad sails. We've gone sailing with him a few times, but he gets so upset with us. We have to sit down and do what he tells us, or he will get mad. We don't go sailing anymore; it's too stressful for us kids. Instead, I like to body surf, catching the waves before they break and letting them carry me to shore. I put my hands together over my head like I am diving. I am so free! It's the closest thing to flying like a bird. I don't have a care in the world. I am bodysurfing with Jacob where the water is way over my head. Jacob swims like a sea lion.

A big wave crashes down over our heads. I tumble upside down, but I can see the bottom of the ocean. I push off with my feet. I pop up like a spring. When I come up for air, I can't see Jacob. I panic. I submerge my head to look for him. His head pops out, ready to catch another wave, and I smile. *You rascal. Don't scare me like that!* I decide to take the next wave in, and work on my tan. I'm so wiped out that I take a nap on the beach.

* * *

I am meeting many new friends at school, but Nan and I are still inseparable. We hang out all the time with our friends. It's Friday, so we decide to ditch school after lunch and make it a long weekend. We run across the street from our junior high and into the park. I am in seventh grade. We sit around the picnic table and pass a joint. I feel accepted by Nan, and this group of friends. I can tell they like me. They love it when I sing and act goofy. I love it, too. We sit and talk for hours listening to the latest songs on the radio, like "Hotel California" by The Eagles. The lyrics, "I heard the mission bells. This could be heaven, or it could be hell," ring true to me. It feels great, like heaven now. My friends really get a kick out of me. I like being the center of attention. I invite them to come over tomorrow. We'll hang out and maybe play a little basketball.

Dad has been living on his sailboat somewhere in LA for the past few weeks. I think he docks it in San Pedro Harbor near my brother Danial's house. Dad got a contract with the city of Glendale helping them design their streets. He was an aeronautical engineer and designed plane engines. I guess he lost that job, too. I can't keep track of him. Sometimes he's coming, but most of the time, he's going.

My stepmom is either hiding in her room or shopping. I don't know and I don't really care. Nan, Billy, Clint, and I are hanging out in my backyard, it's Saturday. Nan really likes Clint. He's the perfect beach bum with long, blond hair and a tanned body. Billy and I are just good friends, as I am Dick's girl, and everybody knows it. Dick had to work, so he couldn't join us. We are sitting in a circle on the basketball court on the hill in our backyard and passing a bong around. We like to sit up here and smoke, so we can see if anyone is coming. We are acting silly and goofing around. Billy is so cute, with long, brown hair and a great personality. He is pretending to be Tarzan, jumping from the hill onto our roof and then running to the other side of the house. He jumps off the roof and screams, "Ahhh! Ahhh! Ahhh!" like Tarzan. We run down to see if he is okay. He is in a bush laughing his head off.

In the distance I can see my dad is coming home for the weekend, so we hightail it out of our yard before he finds us stoned. My friends know my dad is crazy and who knows what he might do to us? I certainly don't want a replay of the axe incident! We head to Billy's house down the street. His parents are out of town. I love the weekends. I can go anywhere and not come home for days.

We invite a ton of friends to come over for a party. The neighbors are out of town, too. They went to Billy's parents' cabin in the mountains together. He breaks into their house. It's easy; Billy lifts the sliding glass patio door by pressing his hands on the glass and leaning on it with his hips, and then lifts it over the lock on the track. It opens easily. They have a pool table and a full bar. I pour myself my new favorite drink, Irish whisky. I took the bottle my dad had in the cabinet after mom died and drank it. I've been drinking whisky ever since.

I say, "I didn't get this raspy voice drinking Pina Coladas." I like my raspy voice. It makes me feel like I have authority.

Billy says, "I love your voice. It's sexy."

I smile and pour another one. I am getting drunk. I help myself to a bunch of Avon toiletries — fancy soap, shampoo, cosmetics, perfume — you name it. The lady is an Avon salesperson, I guess. I hope she won't miss them. My dad refuses to buy us nice toiletries; we just have the basics — Breck shampoo and cream rinse and Ivory soap. I pass out on the couch while my friends play pool.

I wake up before my friends to see everyone crashed on the floor, couches, and chairs. I grab my trash bag filled with goodies and head home. I am really groggy. I didn't sleep well last night; the house was freezing. I sneak into my room, stash the toiletries under my bed, and lie down. I am hung over and fall asleep quickly. I'm awakened by a knock on my bedroom door.

My dad opens my door, he's with two cops.

Oh, crap! My heart is beating out of my chest. I sit up.

The younger cop asks me, "Where were you last night?

I don't lie. "At my friend's, Billy's house."

The older cop, a gray-haired guy my father's age with a gut, asks me, "Did you go over to the neighbor's house?"

"Yeah, our friend said we could play pool there." What I left out is that I stole a ton of Avon products.

The younger cop asks, "Can I look around?"

"Sure," I say, trying to play it cool, even though my stomach is in knots. I'm just praying they don't look under my bed.

He searches my closet, dresser drawers, and then under my bed and discovers the lotion, make-up, and perfume in a big white trash bag. I should have left it at my friend's place.

The cops look at my dad, and the older cop says to him, "Follow us to the police station."

The younger cop taps my shoulder and says, "Follow us." They escort me out of the house and instruct me to climb into the back seat of the police car. As we drive away, I see the neighbor who gave me Jacob watering her roses. *Crap! There goes my babysitting gig.* I am so afraid my dad is going to kill me or at least scream at me. He waits for the cops to book me, then signs some forms agreeing to appear in court. I don't know what's worse — being arrested or facing my father.

Evidently, someone ratted on me. We duck into my dad's car, neither of us saying a word. He pulls into the 31-Flavors ice cream parlor.

"Want some ice cream?" he asks.

"Sure," I say with my head hanging low. I can't even look at him.

We get out of the car and walk into the store. Dad looks at me with a sad, sorry look on his face. He says, "What flavor?"

"Mint chocolate chip, please."

We sit at the counter facing the window, looking out while eating our ice cream cones in silence. I brace for his harsh words, his punishment, but they never come. I can't believe he doesn't discipline me. I guess he is happy that I am talking again and making new friends. I am so relieved. I can do whatever I want, whenever I want!

When I get home, I breeze past my stepmother watching TV. She has a smirk on her ugly face. She has practically emptied our house of anything that resembles our past. She gave to her kids the dining room table and chairs my dad inherited from his mom. Only a folding table remains in the dining room. The walls and shelves that used to display family photos are bare; she tossed them. The only thing she kept was my mother's wedding ring. I can't believe my dad gave her the diamond band he inherited from his mother. I hate my stepmom. I hide in my room and don't talk to anyone much anymore.

* * *

A few weeks have passed since the arrest incident. I'm in my new room across the hall from my old room feeling bored. I smoke a little pot and feel a burst of creativity.

I'm inspired to jazz up the walls. My grandfather gave me a set of paints when he visited for my mom's birthday. I begin to paint this and that throughout.

The next morning, my dad comes in to wake me for school and looks around. "It feels like I've just walked into a garden."

I scan my room, remembering the fun I had sprucing up my walls. I painted the queen of hearts and the ace of spades on one wall, big flowers with snails crawling on the grass on another and the sun and moon on another wall. I say, "Yeah, it does; doesn't it?"

I don't know what I was thinking; maybe it was the pot. I head to the bathroom to get ready for school. *I can't believe Dad isn't mad at me. I guess he doesn't want to hurt my feelings. It seems like I can do anything at any time, and he doesn't care. If he did, he would discipline me — right?*

A few weeks later, I walk into the Sears store down the street from my school. I need new clothes; I've outgrown everything, and I don't want to ask my dad for new ones. I tell the cashier that my bag broke outside, and I need another one. She gives me a new bag. I go into the girl's department and stuff tons of cool clothes into it. I walk right out of the store with my new clothes. I can't believe how easy it is!

At school, I wear the latest Levi's and Ditto pants and the cutest matching tops. I love the thrill of stealing and, obviously, I am good at it. Word gets out that I can score stuff for my friends. They give me a few bucks to get them the styles and sizes they want. I could actually make a business out of this. This is so great!

On my way out of the store, a good-looking young security guard stops me and asks, "Can I see your receipt?"

I fumble through my bag and say, "I must have left it at the register."

He says, "Show me where you shopped so we can find it."

I head toward the department where I got the clothes.

The security guard walks up to the cashier.

"Did this young lady buy clothes here and leave her receipt?"

"I didn't check her out. I've been here all morning," says the cashier.

He takes me to the security office and calls the police.

"The police will be here shortly to take you to the station," says the security guard.

They arrive and haul me down to the station, where they see I have a previous arrest.

They book me. Last time, I was let off, as I returned the products. Because it was my first arrest, they gave me the benefit of the doubt. I doubt they'll see it that way this time. I feel queasy, like I might get sick.

Dad is on his way down here to pick me up. This time for sure I'll be disciplined. I dread him screaming at me more than I dread the punishment. I see him sign something and giving the officer that booked me a handshake. He walks up to me and says,

"We can go now. Are you hungry?"

"A little." I say with my head hanging low.

"I'm starving!" he says.

He pulls into a Sizzler Steak House. He makes small talk while we are waiting to order about school and sailing, as if I did nothing wrong. I can't believe I'm getting away with this. He used to scream all the time. What's up with that? It feels like he doesn't care. If he did, he would punish me. I guess he just doesn't want to break my heart more than it already is. He probably feels guilty for dropping us in our stepmom's lap and running off to San Pedro to live on his sailboat.

> ***I realize now that I was trying to get my father's attention. I kept raising the bar. I wanted discipline.***

Chapter Seven

Fifteen Going on Twenty

My older brother and three sisters ran as far away from home as possible and started their own lives. I regret not knowing them better. With twelve years between my oldest brother and my younger sister, the age gap makes it nearly impossible.

My father took another job two hours away from us and lives on his sailboat. Why not? He has the kids taken care of — right? Wrong! My stepmom is furious. Even though I don't like her one bit, I can see why my dad leaving her with stepchildren would be upsetting.

It's after 10:00 o'clock on Saturday night, and Meagan, Paul, and I are watching the *Carol Burnett Show*, laughing hysterically. Our stepmom emerges from her room with a scowl, hands me a letter, spins around, and storms back into her bedroom. *This can't be good.* She never leaves her bedroom when we are home. I rip open the letter while Paul and Meagan watch. The letter incident upstages the Carol Burnett show.

I read it aloud in a mocking voice. "I am tired of being your housekeeper, maid, secretary, and chauffeur. You need to move out by Monday."

I stare at the letter, then at Paul and Meagan, and back at the letter. I want to scrunch it up and hurl it across the room or rip it into shreds. "She can't do this to us! We should refuse to leave!"

"Do you think we should call Dad?" Meagan asks.

"Heck no!" says Paul. "He might kick her out. Then we'd be stuck with him."

"You're right," I say. "She can have him! But what will we do? Where will we go?"

Paul says, "My boss at Wienerschnitzel is looking for a roommate. I will talk to him tomorrow at work." Meagan says, "I can stay with my friend Carmen until the dust settles." I say, "I can probably stay with Nan, but I want to get out of here for good, so I probably need a better plan."

The next day, I see the Sunday newspaper on the coffee table. I plop down on the couch and peruse jobs in the classified section. Under Domestic Help there's an ad that reads: *Seeking someone to clean my home and cook in exchange for room and board.* I jump up, grab the phone, and dial the number. My heart is beating right out of my chest as I hear the phone ringing in my ear.

"Hi, I'm calling about the job in the paper."

"Do you have any experience with cleaning and cooking?" he asks.

"I took care of my brother and sister when my mom was dying and did all the cooking and cleaning."

"I'm sorry to hear about your mom. How old are you?"

"Eighteen." I lie. Nothing new. I got a Social Security card when Mom died, so that's not going to be a problem. It is time to escape the horror stories of my past.

"My name is Hank. What's your name?"

"Oh, I'm sorry. My name is Jackie."

Hank says, "When can you start?"

"Right away! What's your address?"

I want to ask him if I can bring my dog Jacob, but I don't want anything to prevent me from getting this job, so I don't. I've got to get out of here. I'm so sad to leave my precious dog behind. It breaks what little heart I have left.

Cleaning and cooking for Hank is a cinch; he's in his twenties and real laid back. He lives close to the beach in a cute craftsman bungalow with shake shingles like the homes in Mystic Seaport. I love living near the beach. I sleep with my window open so I can hear the waves.

Hank's parents own laundromats in the area, and his job is collecting the coins and repairing the machines. He surfs by day and makes the rounds to the laundromats by night. Quite the nice setup he has going. I'm relieved he has not tried to have his way with me. I'm not attracted to him with his shiny red face dotted with acne scars and long blond curly hair. But I really like and trust him. He seems like an angel, at least to me. I ask him if I can take a job in town if I continue to do the housekeeping and cooking.

He says, "Yeah, that's fine, kid."

I bodysurf almost every day. I am like a fish — able to stay in the ocean all day. It's so cold yet invigorating on this hot day. I've gained strength from swimming and I am super tanned. My bleach-blonde hair has grown past my butt. I am officially a beach bum. Life is great! So much better than living with my awful stepmom. The only downside is I miss Jacob so much, but he's with me in spirit.

On my way home, I see a help-wanted sign in the window of a clothing store on Ocean Avenue. I smile and walk in. A guy sits at the counter counting money from the cash register. It's 4:45 p.m., almost closing time.

I introduce myself. "I saw the sign in your window. Is the job still available?" Apparently, he is the owner. He is a sweet guy in his thirties with brown hair, green eyes, and a great smile.

"Do you have any experience in retail?"

"No, but I love clothes and fashion."

"I'll give you a shot. Be here tomorrow at 10 a.m."

I run home and tell Hank.

"Way to go, kid! Let's celebrate with pizza and beer. Take the night off."

One day, a cute guy walks into the store and flirts with me. He says he's Bo from Boise, Idaho, and plays soccer on a traveling team. He seems a little older than I, but I don't care. I flirt back.

"Would you like to swing by my hotel after work? Our team just won against the Ocean Beach boys. We're going to celebrate."

I smile real big in my sexy yellow halter dress and flip my hair back. "That sounds fun."

"We'll be hanging out at the pool. See you later," he says, smiling back.

You can tell he's super athletic by his buff body — trim and strong. And his smile melts my heart. It's beating fast like it's going to beat right out of my chest.

Nobody has been in the store for over an hour. I lock up early around 4:30. Before I head out, I grab a yellow string bikini from the rack and shove it into my purse. A gentle breeze tickles my skin and the bright sunshine warms my face. I have a skip in my step as I head for the Ocean Beach Hotel. I spot Bo by the pool. There's a girl on a lounge chair next to him. His buddies are in the pool tossing a football around. They stop and smile as I walk past them. I plunk down onto the lounge chair next to Bo.

He jumps up and gives me a hug. "I'm glad you came." We chat for a few minutes and then he dives into the pool to join the football game.

I smile at the girl in the lounge chair. "Hi, I'm Jackie."

"Hi! I'm Deirdre." She has an accent I can't place.

"Are you from here?" I ask.

"I was living in Jersey until my mom rescued me from the foster-care system a few days ago. My mom is a Las Vegas showgirl, or so she says. I think she's really a stripper." She laughs. "I don't care. I can't wait to go to Las Vegas with her tomorrow."

Deirdre is like me — 15 going on 20. She also had a rough start. She told me her mom got hooked on drugs, and Social Services put her in foster care in New Jersey where they were living at the time. I feel a special connection to her.

"Can I go to your room and put on my suit?"

"For sure. Let's go." She turns to the guys in the pool and says, "We'll be right back. Jackie needs to put on her suit."

Bo hollers, "Hurry back!"

We walk upstairs to her room. There's a note on the bed and a hundred bucks. She picks up the note and starts to cry.

"What's is it?"

Deirdre says, "I guess I'm not going to Vegas. My mom ditched me. She says in the note, 'I don't know how to be a mom.' It's kind of true, but she's the only mom I have."

I am shocked. *How could her mom do this? I mean, stepmoms do it, but real moms? That's harsh.* I give her a big hug. "Don't worry. You can stay with me."

She stops crying. "Really? That would be awesome. I don't have anywhere to go."

"I cook and clean for a guy in exchange for a room. I'll ask if you can share my room."

"I thought you worked at a clothing store," she says.

"Yeah, I do, but I just got the job. You can help me clean and cook for him. He's cool. You'll like Hank."

She says, "Let's go to the pool and party. Don't tell the guys my mom left me here, please."

"Don't worry. Your secret's safe with me."

We head back to the pool and plunge in. The guys splash water on us. We are laughing our heads off. It's fun acting silly with them. We jump out after we are thoroughly waterlogged and recline in our lounge chairs. Bo hands each of us a cold beer. The first sip is so refreshing. We stick around for a little while longer and then tell the guys we will be back later. I want to take Deirdre to meet Hank.

Bo says with his big white smile, "Hurry back."

I hope Hank is okay with her staying with us. Otherwise, I don't have a Plan B. We walk into the house and he is lying on the couch watching TV.

"Hi Hank! This is my girlfriend, Deirdre. I was wondering if it would be all right if she stayed here with us for a while. With me working at the store, she can cook and clean during the day."

"Sure, as long as you're okay with sharing your room."

I give him a big hug and say, "Thank you! You're the best!"

Deirdre looks relieved. She says, "Thanks, Hank. I'll take care of everything."

We fix him a hamburger and chips while he is watching football.

I hand him his meal and say, "See ya later." We head back to the hotel to gather Deirdre's stuff and party with the guys.

It's great having Deirdre at Hank's. She lightens my workload by doing most of the cleaning and all the cooking while I am at work. When she's finished with her work, she hangs out at the beach. Together, we dream of becoming models, maybe even actresses. Coincidentally, she met a photographer at the beach who said he could photograph our portfolios. We are elated.

She says, "He wants us to do a few nude shots, too. If you don't mind."

I say, "Who cares? I don't."

She giggles. I love her laugh. It reminds me of Nan. I miss her.

I laugh with her and jump around, imagining our bright futures. "Maybe we can be Playboy Bunnies for Hugh."

We catch the bus to the photographer's house the next day after work. We have our clothes in Deirdre's suitcase ready for our photo sessions. She knows right where to go. She obviously has been here before.

Paul is a short, chubby nerd and much older — possibly in his thirties. He wears thick coke-bottle glasses that distort his eyes.

I pose for a few nude shots. It doesn't faze me in the least. The only troubling thing is if Paul thinks we're going to sleep with him. There's no way I will. He gives me the creeps. It's possible Deirdre already did, but I don't ask. I am just happy she scored free photoshoots to launch our modeling and acting careers. I imagine myself posing on the red carpet once my acting career has taken off!

A few days later, we return to Paul's house, and he presents us with a beautiful album filled with 8x10 shots. As I page through it, I can see he is very good at what he does. We hang out with him for a little while. He is seemingly harmless. Who cares if he gets a kick taking pictures of young girls naked? I got a portfolio out of the deal. My years of performing around the piano with mom will pay off. I am destined for stardom!

Paul invites us to go to the California Jam II concert in L.A. The Jam Concerts are the Woodstock of the 70s. I had heard the first Jam was great.

I say, "Hell yeah!" and Deirdre echoes me.

He says, "I'll drive."

We are so excited that we are headed for the big city of L.A. The concert is scheduled for tomorrow night, March 10, 1978, at 7:00 p.m. at the Ontario Speedway. I'll be 16 on April 18th, so we'll celebrate my birthday a month early.

We tell Hank we are going to LA for the weekend.

He says, "Have fun! It should be a great concert."

Paul pulls up to the house at 10 a.m. We run out when we hear his horn. He's driving a converted van with a bed in the back. On the side is a graphic of a naked lady with black long hair covering her body.

I jump in the back and Deirdre takes the passenger seat. She says, "Let the good times roll! Rock and roll, that is!"

Paul gets on the freeway heading north and we drive for a few hours. I help myself to a beer in the minifridge. We pull up to a huge outdoor camping area with a big stage in the front. He hands the guy at the gate our tickets and we drive in and park.

We set up some folding chairs outside the van and drink another beer. The lineup is great: Aerosmith, Heart, Foreigner, and Bob Welch, just to name a few. I love the Foreigner songs, "*It Feels Like the First Time*" and "*Cold as Ice*." I can relate. Even though I haven't had a first time, other than being raped, which I don't remember, I am cold as ice. One day, I will have a first time. I can't wait to be in love for the first time!

Paul rolls a joint and passes it to me.

Deirdre says, "I'll be back. I need to use the restroom."

She's been gone awhile. I tell Paul I'm going to walk around to see if I can find her.

He says, "Sure. I'll leave the van unlocked, if I go anywhere."

I find her with some biker guys, and we hang out for a while. Their tent is set up by the restrooms. They are much older than we are, but everyone here is much older. Deirdre tells me she is going to stay in LA with Jay, the biker dude, for the weekend.

I say, "Don't do anything I wouldn't do!" and laugh.

I head back to the van. Paul is already asleep in the bed. I sit outside in the chair and fall asleep after the concert is over. In the morning, Paul asks me, "Did you ever find Deirdre?"

I say, "Yeah, she is going to stay here with some guy she met."

He rolls his eyes. "Whatever."

We pack up the van and drive back to Ocean Beach. He doesn't say much the whole way back. I think he is ticked off at Deirdre.

He pulls up to Hank's house. "See ya around," I say.

Deirdre calls that night. "Guess what? Jay has a four-bedroom house. We can live here while we look for modeling jobs."

I am finally going to get a break from scrubbing dirty toilets. It is time for me to spread my wings and fly. I give my notice at the store and tell Hank I am moving to LA. I am so excited to start my new life in the big city of Los Angeles!

I call home the next day. Meagan answers. "How are you? We've been so worried about you."

"Don't worry. I'm great. I'm moving to LA tomorrow. My friend has a house there."

She says, "I can't believe you're moving to LA. I've missed you so much. I came back home after staying at my friend's place for a week. Dad came home for the weekend and wanted to see me. He asked Lucille where you were, and she said you ran away. I couldn't tell him the truth because I didn't want to be kicked out again."

"Promise me you won't tell him. I don't want him to divorce her. Then you'll be stuck with him! She can have him."

Meagan says, "I won't. Promise me you'll stay in touch. I worry about you when I don't hear from you."

"I promise."

I miss Meagan and Paul. I hope he's okay.

I say good-bye to Hank and thank him so much for understanding.

He says, "Don't worry about it. I'll be fine. Just take care of yourself, will ya?"

I take a cab to the Greyhound Bus station. My bus leaves for LA in an hour. I am sitting here thinking, *I hope I don't regret this. I really like it here.* A voice over the loudspeaker announces that the bus for LA is boarding, so I grab my suitcase and walk to an empty seat in the back by the bathroom. We take off a few minutes later.

Looking out the window, I see my life pass in front of me. I say goodbye to San Diego. We pass through National City where mom is buried. I see the exit and say good-bye to her in my heart. Who knows when I will be back? When I arrive at the station, Jay is there to pick me up in his friend's car. He is a rough-looking guy with long red hair, a straggly beard, and a mustache. He's dressed in a black T-shirt and his arms are covered with tattoos. I guess he's in his forties, maybe fifties, because he has grey in his beard. Who knows? He has bad teeth and smokes like a chimney. His eyes are bloodshot; he looks high. I'm not thrilled about going with him, but I want to see Deirdre.

He says, "Hi, kid. Deirdre is at home making lunch." He grabs my suitcase and I follow him to the car.

We walk into a '70s ranch-style house that reminds me of my dad's place. When I walk in, I see my girlfriend being thrown against a wall by a crazy biker bitch. She is a tough-looking broad — very overweight with lots of tattoos. She's wearing a navy-blue bandana on her head and looks like she just got off her motorcycle.

She screams, "Get this bitch out of here now or I will call the police for the warrant you have for murder."

I am in shock! *What?! Did Jay murder someone?*

Deirdre pries herself off the floor. She's wide-eyed and a bit disoriented, but she's okay. Thank God. I can see fear in Jay's eyes. He grabs Deirdre, we jump into his roommate's car, and drive north on the 405 freeway. I have nowhere to go, so I guess I'm going wherever Jay is driving us. I don't think he is going to hurt us, but who knows? Maybe he got in a fight with someone at a bar and it got out of control. I don't ask, nor does Deirdre. We don't want to know the details. I wish I would have asked my little sister for my older siblings' phone numbers.

Fuck you God. Is this your idea of a joke? Ha! Ha! What more can you do to screw up my life? First my mom, then my stepmom, now I'm with a guy wanted for murder. I lift my hand up toward the sky and give God the finger.

Jay says, "Don't worry, guys. I have a friend in Oregon. We just need to get over the border before the police find me."

I don't say anything. I just hang my head down. *So much for finding a modeling job. Another dream crushed. What else is new?* I roll a joint, take a hit, and pass it to Deirdre.

Deirdre and I exchange wide-eyed looks but don't say anything. I'm filled with dread and trepidation. It looks like I am going along for the ride. We've been driving all day and night. I fall asleep wishing I never listened to Deirdre.

We arrive in Beaverton, a town outside of Portland, around 3:00 a.m. . Jay pulls up to an old gas station that seems like it's abandoned. A guy who looks like he was just released from prison approaches our car. Jay jumps out and gives him a big hug. He has long brown hair peppered with gray. He is dressed in a sleeveless, blue-plaid flannel shirt and holey blue jeans. He is covered with tattoos like the one's prisoners have — black and colorless.

Deirdre and I climb out of the car. Jay introduces us. The guy's smile reveals that he has stained, crooked teeth. He gives Deirdre a hug and then me. I feel nauseous from his putrid odor; it smells like he hasn't showered in a month.

Jay's friend lives behind the gas station he manages. He takes us to his house, so we can settle in. As we approach the house, I notice a few of the windows are boarded up. I have a pit in my stomach. When we walk in, the stench of stale smoke and beer permeates the air. I try not to breathe. I put my suitcase down and look around. Dirty dishes and old pizza boxes with chewed-up crust and empty beer bottles are scattered everywhere. It smells like old garbage. I can't believe anyone lives here.

Jay's friend shouts, "Shut the fuck up!" to the back yard where two barking Dobermans are behind a six-foot chain-link fence topped with barbwire. *Like anyone would jump over the fence with dogs who look like they could kill you with one bite.*

I need to go to the bathroom, but I'm afraid what I will discover. It's even worse than I imagined. The toilet is black, with piss all over the floor and mildewed dirty towels that look like they could stand up in a corner. I don't sit down on the toilet to pee. *Shit! There's no toilet paper*. So, I drip dry. I can't believe this is my life now. I want to cry, but I suck it up and act unfazed when I return to the living room.

I sit down on the couch that looks like it should be on the side of the road, or better yet in a dump. I roll a joint. I need to get high. *What the hell am I doing here? Thanks, God! You're funny.* I feel totally abandoned.

The next day, Deirdre and I clean the house from top to bottom. It's Sunday, so the gas station is closed. For the next few weeks, we work as cashiers at the gas station, as it also has a small convenience store.

On Friday night, we decide to get some steaks and beer for a barbeque. I give Deirdre 40 bucks. When I tell her to get me some Jack Daniels, she smiles. She and Jay head to the store. I tell her not to steal anything. She gives me an evil smirk like she just might. I know she likes the thrill of stealing.

When Jay came home without her, I ask, "Where's Deirdre?"

"She stole some Visine in the checkout line and the cashier called the police when she denied it. The police arrived quickly, so I headed back here."

"Damn, her. I told her not to steal anything!"

I can't believe he just left her there. What was he thinking? That prick!

Deirdre calls the gas station from the police station. She says, "They found the Visine I took, and a joint in my purse. I told them I was seventeen, which I thought was old enough to be on my own."

"No, stupid. You need to be eighteen. Damn you, Deirdre! I told you not to steal anything."

She says, "I know. What can I say? I fucked up. They are sending me back into the foster-care system, because I don't have a clue about how to reach my mom. I'll call you when I get there. Please send me a fake ID, so I can run away and come back here."

"I will. I promise."

I stay up late drinking Jack Daniels. I'm in this godforsaken house with a so-called murderer and his drug-addict friends. A dealer drops by to bring them crack. I can't shoot up myself, so Jay puts a tourniquet on my arm while I look away. As soon as he extracts the needle, I run to the bathroom and throw up. As I lie on the floor, the room is spinning. I feel like I am in hell. *God if I live, I will never shoot drugs up again.* I get a whiff of the urine on the floor and throw up again. I can't understand how crack is supposed to be a good thing. I'm done with it.

The guys pretty much leave me alone to do my own thing. Thankfully, they haven't tried to get me in bed, yet. They need me more than I need them to clean the house, cook, and work the cash register. Believe it or not, I've become friends with Ed, the drug dealer. He doesn't use, either. Ed notices that I am not shooting up.

"Hey, do you want to get out of here?

"What do you think?"

"I have a friend who's looking for a roommate."

"I have a few bucks left but not enough for a room."

"She can get you a job where she works."

"Hell, yeah! Get me out of this hellhole!"

I pack my bag while the guys are strung out on the crack they just shot up. Ed grabs my suitcase and takes me to his friend's two-bedroom apartment. Her sister lives there, too.

She says, "You can sleep on the couch."

"Hey, thanks a lot. I appreciate it." I sit down on the couch (aka: my bed) and roll a joint. Ed, the drug dealer, hands her a bag of crack.

I look at her. "I've got this. It's the least I can do." I hand him 40 bucks.

"Do you want the first hit?" she asks.

"No, thanks. It's all yours."

I can't bear seeing me in these unimaginable places. I remember how closed off I had become. I hardened my heart. I swore I would never open my heart to anyone ever again. Maybe mom's trying to tell me that it's safe for me to open my heart now, undo that promise.

Chapter Eight

Sixteen Going on Twenty-Five

My new roommates, Shawn and Jessica, are nude models. Shawn takes me to meet their boss. It's in seedy part of town not far from the gas station. It's a standalone building but there are other businesses like it on the same street. We walk through the lobby and down a dark hall into her boss's office in the back of the building. There's a bed in here.

I shoot her a weird look.

She whispers, "He spends the night here occasionally." She then says, "Kevin, this is Jackie. She's my new roomie. Can you use another model? She has a portfolio." She rolls her eyes at me.

When I show the boss my photo album, he hires me on the spot. Little did I know he would hire anyone who was willing. I thought I needed to convince him. I guess that is why Shawn rolled her eyes. He takes the composite sheet out of the album side pocket, which features little photos on an 8x10 sheet and one of the nude 8x10 shots.

He looks at them and says, "Do you have a driver's license or other identification?"

He catches me off guard. I stutter, "Uh, no, I lost it."

He says, "I'll make you one with this headshot. I'll need to take 50 bucks out of your first paycheck."

I say, "Sure, that would be great. Can you make one for my girlfriend, too? I can bring you her headshot tomorrow."

He smiles. "Sure. Is she looking for a job?"

"Yeah, but she is out of town for a few weeks. I'll bring her in when she comes back."

The next night, Shawn takes me with her to work. Kevin slides the nude shots from my portfolio into a photo album of nude girls that customers page through. There are Polaroid cameras behind the desk and some film on the desk, along with a For Sale sign.

He says, "Do you have a nightie?"

I say, "Yeah, it's in my purse."

He says, "Go put it on and wait in the kitchen for a customer."

Shawn shows me to the bathroom. The nude photographer studio is an awful place where random guys enter dark rooms with you. They can't touch me, but they can photograph me with a Polaroid camera.

Things have gone from bad to worse. I am totally checked out and feel like a lost cause. Kevin walks into the kitchen. "Jackie, you have a customer."

He walks me into a dark room with a single black vinyl bed in the corner and a chair next to it. He says, "Take off your nightie when the customer comes in. I'll be in the closet outside, which has a two-way mirror to make sure the guy doesn't touch you."

I say, "Sure. Thanks."

The customer walks in and says, "Hi."

I slip off the little black nighty my roommate gave me and lie down on the couch. He stands over me and asks me to pose.

I put my arm over my head and lean up and say, "Do what you gotta do. What you see is what you get."

He's a heavy-set guy who barely fits in the chair next to the bed. He whips out his dick to jack off. I squeeze my eyes closed. There's an awful smell, so I open my eyes to see cum all over him. I get up, hand him some baby wipes, put my nighty on and walk out. I feel so humiliated and totally defiled. I walk into the breakroom and light a cigarette. I inhale deeply, hoping the nicotine will numb the pain.

My boss walks in and hands me the two ID cards.

I call Jay at the service station the next day and ask him if he has heard from Deirdre.

He says, "Yeah, she's in a foster home in Jersey. She wants me to come get her."

"I got her a fake ID. Do you have her address so I can send it to her?"

"Yeah, hold on. I'll get it."

A week later, after I get paid, I mail Deirdre the ID with a letter saying I can get her a job. I give her my address and phone number. I slip a hundred bucks in the envelope and tell her to take the Greyhound here. I can't wait to see her!

Shawn and Jessica are hooked on crack and heroin. They have needle marks lining their arms. They lie on the couch after they use and don't say much. They don't throw up like I did when I tried it at Jay's. They get loaded every night after work. I guess I can't blame them.

When I came home from work tonight, the neighbor lady is sitting on the steps smoking a cigarette. She tells me that Jessica overdosed and died. Apparently, she found her on the floor in the laundry room and called an ambulance. I'm in shock. I can't believe she isn't here. Even though I didn't know her well, I really liked Jessica. She was a sweet soul. Now Shawn is at the morgue, identifying her body. No wonder she ran out of work without saying anything.

The only way I am going to survive this is to keep closing myself off from the world. That way I won't have to feel anything. I am numb. I roll a joint. I need to get high. Hopefully, Jessica is in a better place. This can't be all there is.

Shawn walks in.

I say, "Oh, Shawn, I'm so sorry."

She says, "I don't want to talk about it," walks into her bedroom and slams the door.

A week later Deirdre calls me ecstatically. "I'll be there in a few days!"

Our boss at the jack-off parlor, so-called Nude Photography Studio, requires all the girls to sleep with him. One of the models is his girlfriend, Joan. I like her. She is a real cool chick and pretty, too. She has long brown curly hair and a very curvy body, like mine. I am getting sexy and have an hour-glass figure, but I'm still slender. I refuse to sleep with that prick. I've only been here a few months and have completely avoided him.

Deirdre arrived today. She's so happy to be here and doesn't want Jay to know she's here.

I tell her, "Don't worry. Everything is going to be all right. I won't tell him."

Shawn is okay with her staying here. I take Jessica's room, even though it's a little creepy to sleep in a dead girl's room. Deirdre crashes on the couch. It's good to have her back. I feel like we are sisters, in a way. We take her to work that night. Our boss hires her on the spot. She doesn't mind sleeping with him. She thinks it's the least she can do for a job and freedom.

Kevin says, "Meet me in the back room after your session." The back room is his bedroom where he fucks girls.

I glare at him and say, "Fuck off!"

"If you don't want to pay up, you can get out of here. I don't need your shit!"

"I don't care. I don't need this shit!"

I storm out, happy to be free from the jack-off parlor.

Deirdre asks me later when she gets home, "What are you going to do?"

"One of my customers has been trying to get me to work for a friend. His friend is an old lady that wants me to sleep with her supposed friends/customers. She'll split the money with me and give me a room in her house. You can have my room. I haven't been able to sleep in there anyway, ever since Jessica died."

She says, "Are you sure you want to do this? I'm worried about you."

"Don't worry. I'll be fine. I promise. If I am going to sleep with some prick, I may as well be getting paid for it."

The next day, my client picks me up at Shawn's house and drives me to his friend's house.

He introduces us, "Evelyn, this is Jackie. I've gotta go to work. I'll see you later."

She shows me to my bedroom. The décor is fifties' style with antique white and gold furniture and godawful wallpaper with gold flowers. Evelyn is in her sixties, maybe even seventies.

"We've got a customer coming over soon. Get ready!"

As I wait, I think, "What am I supposed to do?" I have never had sex while conscious. I roll a joint and get high and then light up a cigarette, so Evelyn won't smell the pot. There is a knock at the door. An old skinny bald guy walks up to me sitting on the bed and takes off my clothes. I have a pit in my stomach. It's hard to breathe. I don't know what to do, so I take off my bra and panties as he undresses and lie down on the bed. He crawls on top of me and sticks his hard cock in my pussy. It hurts like hell. I close my eyes and cry, but he doesn't notice.

He says, "You're tight." There's a jar of Vaseline on the bed table. He takes some out and puts it on my pussy.

I don't say anything. I just let him fuck me. What else can I do? He is on top of me, his sweat drips all over my body. I feel like I might puke. Thankfully, it doesn't take long before he's done.

He gets up and gets dressed. I go to the bathroom and take a shower to cleanse myself of him and to wash off the putrid smell. When I come out of the bathroom, I see $40 sitting on the dresser. I crawl into bed and I cry myself to sleep. I wake up at 7:15 a.m. and see only twenty bucks on the dresser. Apparently, Evelyn took her cut. Twenty dollars in exchange for my dignity doesn't seem the least bit fair.

I head to the kitchen and Evelyn asks if I want some coffee.

I say, "Yes, please." There is nothing to say.

She makes me some eggs and toast. "Get ready. We have a busy day ahead of us."

My client from the nude photography studio who got me this job, comes over while I am eating breakfast . I thought he was coming over to say hi. Evidently, he's my next customer. I should have known that's why he got me this job. He wants to sleep with me. Overcome with dread, I walk out without saying a word.

A few minutes later, there's a knock on my bedroom door. I have nothing to say to him, so I take off my clothes and lay down. It is a repeat performance of the night before. He says he will be back in a few days. No money is exchanged. I guess this one is on the house. That fucker! I can't trust anyone, especially not anyone from the male species. They are all fuckers. I hate men. I feel so alone and betrayed by God.

Thanksgiving Day arrives and Evelyn is having some friends over. She tells me to take the day off. I try to reach Deirdre at the house. No one answers, so I walk down the street to a Kentucky Fried Chicken to get some lunch. I am so lonely and miss my family terribly. I haven't seen them for nearly a year. I walk into a phone booth and call directory assistance for my grandfather's number. He is my rock. I love him so much. He always makes me smile. I want to smile today. Mom died four years ago on Thanksgiving. My Uncle Bill, my godfather, who has the same name as my grandfather, answers the phone. Apparently, the operator gave me his number instead.

He says, "Call home immediately. Your brother Paul has third-degree burns from the waist up and they don't know if he will ever use his hands again."

"Oh my God! What happened?"

"Honey, I don't know all the details. Please call home. Everyone has been so worried about you."

How can this be happening? Paul is an incredible piano player; he needs his hands to play. God, how can you do this to him? First my mother's death and now my brother's hands? I hate you, God!

I call home immediately.

Meagan answers the phone on the first ring. "Oh, Jackie, I thought you were the hospital calling. We have been worried sick about you. Please come home. Paul is at the Scripps Institute in San Diego. He is out of critical care and will come home soon."

I say, "Uncle Bill told me. What happened?"

"He had an accident at work."

"I'll be home soon. I promise."

I must swallow my pride. Even though I never want to see my stepmom again, I am going to see my family.

One of my clients is a truck driver who has agreed to give me a lift. There are still some good men in the world even though he pays to sleep with me. He must care enough about me to get me the fuck out of this godforsaken place. He doesn't make a move on me. We just talk the whole way.

He stops in front of the hospital. "Take care of yourself. You're better than this."

He is an angel in a way. Maybe a black angel, but an angel, nonetheless.

I rush into the hospital and ask the gal at the front desk about Paul.

She says, "He's in Room 307. Take the elevator to the third floor."

I walk into Paul's room and am stopped dead in my tracks. His eyes are shut, like he's sleeping. He is hooked up to an EKG machine. He looks like a mummy; his head, neck, torso and arms are wrapped in dressing. I stand by his bedside gently touching his shoulder.

He opens his eyes. "Is that really you or am I dreaming?"

I try to smile even though I am so sad inside. I say, "It's really me. How are you?"

He says, "I never knew this kind of pain existed, but it is worth it to have you back."

I'm so touched. I love him so much. *I can't believe he said it was worth the pain to have me back.* I am connected to him, mind, body, and soul. I start to give him a hug but decide it might hurt him. We talk for a while. He tells me dad is picking me up to take me home.

My dad strolls in, glances at me.

"Hi, Paul. I'm taking Jackie home with me." Then he looks at me and says, "Let's go."

I can't believe he doesn't even ask where I've been. I look at Paul with weary eyes.

"I'll be home in a few days. We can catch up then," says Paul.

Dad tells me on the way home that they found a good home for Jacob. I don't say anything. I am sure my stepmom got rid of him. I am crushed. I really wanted to see him. *Why is it that anyone I love goes away?*

My stepmom prepared a dinner of canned ham and green beans, and macaroni and cheese from a box. I am starving, so I sit down to eat, even though the dinner looks unappetizing. It's so good to see Meagan. I have missed her like crazy. She is talking a mile a minute.

Thank God, because I don't have much to say. No one even asks me where I've been.

I ask, "So, what happened exactly?"

Meagan says, "There was an explosion at Paul's work when he was working on a forklift. The propane tank valve got stuck and exploded. He was rushed to the hospital. A miracle occurred that day. I prayed to God to please spare him. Paul is a walking miracle. The doctors said he will be all right!" She continues saying in a less enthusiastic tone, "They had other patients with more severe injuries that did not get their mobility back. This is the second largest burn institute in the world, so he is getting the best care, paid for by his company. Because it's a work-related injury, he will get a cash settlement. They are releasing him tomorrow, I think."

It feels weird to be home. I thought I would never return. Thank God Dad is at work every day, so I don't have to see him much. My stepmom is mostly in her room. She is avoiding me. I am sure she doesn't want to talk about my departure from this place.

My grandfather calls and tells me that he's going to buy Paul and me plane tickets to go visit them on the East Coast. I can't wait!

My father went to pick up Paul from the hospital. They come home an hour or so later. Paul looks weary but relieved to be home. He still lives with his old boss at the fast-food restaurant he worked at before he got this job. Paul needs help with his wounds, so he shows me how to change his dressings. It's easy, but it breaks my heart to see his burns.

He says, "It doesn't hurt much anymore. I'll be okay. I'm just so happy you're back. We're going to have a blast on the East Coast." We are leaving tomorrow.

We hop on a plane and make the five-hour journey to Rhode Island. Our relatives welcome us with open arms. When they see Paul, they say that they have been praying tirelessly. The plan is to stay with them for a few days and then go visit our cousin in Boston on way to our Aunt's home in Connecticut.

Every morning after breakfast, Grandpa and Grandma sit in their living room and go through their rosary beads. I hear them repeating "Our Father's" and "Hail Mary's" religiously. It feels so good to be here in this safe place with them. We have the most incredible visit with Mom's siblings — our aunts and uncles. They shower us with love. We are Mary's kids, after all, who they loved and adored. Grandpa and Mom's sister Florence were the only ones who saw her before she died.

Paul and I catch a train to Boston to go visit our cousin. Gazing out the windows in the dining car while sipping whisky , my whole life flashes in front of me, like a movie. So much has happened in the 10 years since we left the East Coast. It saddens me to think I am not the same innocent little girl. She is lost forever. I think about Deirdre and pray she's okay. I will probably never see her again. I am not going back to that life. Bob Seger's song, "*Turn the Page*," plays in my head.

It's mid-December and cold outside. There is snow piled up along the railroad tracks from the past few months and smoke spiraling out of the chimneys. I am relieved to be here where it's safe, feeling warm in my heart next to my brother. He is an archangel who saved me. At least temporarily.

We get off the train and walk into a bar at Quincy Market Place Station where our cousin is going to meet us. There is a long wooden bar with several empty stools. It's late afternoon and everyone is still working. We sit down at the bar and order a few drinks before our cousin gets off work. Paul can move his bandaged arms and fingers. He looks good, considering. He has some scarring on his face, but not much. It must have been a miracle. I say to myself, *Thank you, Lord, for taking care of my brother. I owe you that.* For a minute, I'm a little less angry with God.

The bartender, Jamie, is so cute; he's tall and thin with green eyes and brown hair. He is Irish, of course. I am not old enough to drink. You must be 18 to drink legally in the East Coast. I am only 17, but I look 25. Jamie serves us drinks while I talk about how well Paul can play the piano.

He says, "There's a grand piano on the balcony, go play something for us."

Paul shrugs it off and gets up. "I'm going to the bathroom."

A few minutes later, I hear the boogie woogie from the balcony. Tears are billowing up in my eyes, rolling down my cheeks and into my mouth. I can taste the salt, but it feels like honey to my soul. I see the rays from the sun coming in through the window. I don't dare turn around to look, for fear he will stop. I thank the Lord for hearing my prayer to heal my brother's hands so he could play the piano again. I can't believe what I am hearing. God heard my cry and granted me a miracle. The doctors weren't sure he would get his mobility back enough to play again. How can He still love me enough to hear my prayer after how awful I have been? *Thank you, Lord. I do love you. Thank you for loving me, even though I don't love myself. I feel your love right now. It is so healing to bask in your Grace and Mercy and listen to Paul play the piano.* I feel our mother here, too. The music stops, and Paul comes down from the balcony with a smirk on his face. We hug. I start crying some more. This is a miracle! My mother is pulling strings with God in heaven today.

After a nice visit with my cousin, Paul and I take the train to visit our dad's sister, Aunt Laurie. She prepared a wonderful home-cooked meal of pot roast with carrots and potatoes. Paul is leaving in the morning to go back to California. She asks me to stay with her. She is a nurse at Yale Hospital. Her husband was a surgeon there and died a few years ago. I call home after dinner and talk to my dad about it.

He says, "I have already spoken to her. It will be good for you."

I am living in a beautiful, large, turn-of-the-century home with my aunt, who's a stranger to me. It's furnished with French provincial furniture and fine art like my dad's mom's home. My bedroom looks like something out of a movie set — very charming. My aunt is tall and very pretty for an older lady. She is in her mid-fifties, I think, and wears formal clothes that are very conservative. She has the same mannerisms as my dad's mom and the same condescending way towards me. She's always correcting my vocabulary, manners, and clothes. I can tell she thinks she is doing me a favor, and I guess she is. My mother's family is so down-to-earth, but not my father's. They are so matter of fact and judgmental. Thankfully, my aunt has some pull in this community, as I only had to take a few tests to be placed in the right grade.

I go to school in high heels. I notice that the other girls wear Topsider shoes, khaki pants, and oxford shirts. My aunt takes me shopping over the weekend to buy the proper wardrobe. I am happy that she cares enough to show me the way to act, talk, and dress. It feels good for a change that someone cares about me. I am excelling in school. I love it. I really do. I wish I could stay here to finish high school. I am 17 and in the eleventh grade, but I feel 30. I have been chewed up and spit out by the cold, harsh world. Some of the kids think I am a substitute teacher. With my new wardrobe and mannerisms, I learn to blend in with the upper-class kids who lead sheltered lives. It is a great adventure acting like a kid again, even though I don't feel like one of them.

My dad is coming to get me when school lets out in a few days. I wish I could stay here, but at the same time I am excited to go home. I feel like an outcast here.

* * *

Nothing has changed, now that I am home. I hate my stepmom and my dad is still checked out. I call the owner of the clothing store to see if I can get my old job back. He says his friend Sharon has a room for rent and she can get me a job. I met Sharon when I was working at his clothing store in Ocean Beach. She is older than me — probably in her twenties.

She says she is an escort and can get me some clients. I can't believe I have such bad luck. But I don't care. I just need to get out of this house.

Sharon's business is called California Girls. She placed an ad in an adult magazine that advertises escorts. All she has to do is plug the phone in when she needs money and the phone rings off the hook.

Sharon is a pretty, curvy blonde who looks like she's been ridden hard and put away wet. Her face shows signs of too much sun and not enough sleep. She drinks too much and sleeps with any guy who will have her, which is too many, in my opinion.

Sharon and I go to high-end hotels together when we're working. I wait for her while she is in a client's hotel room, and, in turn, she waits for me when I am servicing a client. Many of the customers are my father's age. Some of them are younger and good looking. The men order room-service and good champagne. I guess they don't want serious relationships with girls, or they just want easy sex, so they hire call-girls.

I'm empty inside. *Is this all I am worth?* I disconnect whenever I have sex with my clients. I still have never had an orgasm. I wonder what it feels like to be in love and enjoy sex. I don't want a boyfriend, not if I'm doing this. But I am making great money and we are scoring backstage passes to rock concerts in San Diego. Sharon knows the stage manager at the sports arena.

It is great going to backstage parties where we meet and party with the band members. I met Tom Petty last week and tonight we are at ZZ Top's backstage party. I am on top of the world, or so I think. I shop at the most expensive stores and have a gorgeous wardrobe. I get my hair styled at the best salons in town. I am a knock-out, too. I have learned to use that to my advantage. And, all the while, I have mastered the art of not feeling anything.

One day, Sharon gets busted in a hotel room by an undercover cop. He says he will let her off if I help them take down the largest prostitution company in the area.

I am at the police station where she is being held.

The head guy with the vice squad says, "We don't want you guys. You're small operators. We want your competition."

They're after a big prostitution operation called Surfer Girls. We know the guy who owns it. He is a prick. Sharon used to work for him. He is always asking me to come work for him. I would never in a million years. I know that he will call the shots and try to use and abuse me. Fuck him!

I say, "Sure, I'll cooperate. Just tell me what to do."

"Come by tomorrow around 2:00 o'clock." He puts his card on the table and leaves.

I can't let Sharon stay locked up. There's no choice but to cooperate with the police. I go to the police station at 2:00 the next day. A guy who works there wires me up. They have me call the guy who owns Surfer Girls.

"Hey, this is Jackie. I'd like to speak with you in person," I say.

"Oh, hi! Come on over."

The front office gal shows me into his office. He is sitting with a shit-eating grin behind a big desk. He looks like the devil in disguise. He is an older guy in his fifties. He is tanned with pearly white teeth. His designer clothes are way too tight. It's clear he's feeling good that I am finally willing to work for him. I'm a little nervous so I put on a confident veneer.

When we're alone in his office, I say, "Sharon's a bitch. I want to be on my own."

He is acting so smug, like I need him. "If you want to make real money, I can do that for you. I have the best clients who will pay you big money to go out with them."

"What do they want me to do with them?" I play dumb.

"What do you think? They want young girls like you to sleep with them. They pay big money for the young ones."

He knows I am underage. He promises to bring me all the best paying customers, if I can make them feel young again.

I want to shut him down, so I say, "I can get you lots of underage girls. I'll make you loads of money; I promise."

"The more you can bring me, the more money you'll get. I will give you a bigger piece of the pie."

I smile and extend my hand to seal the deal with a handshake. "You've got a deal. I'll see you tomorrow."

I was so afraid, but he walked right into the trap. I leave his office and walk down the street where the head of the vice squad is in a van.

He says, "Well done." He removes the wire. "You're free to go now."

"What about Sharon?"

"I'll call the station and tell them to let her go."

I did it! It was scary as hell, yet exciting. I nailed the competition! I am good at the art of the deal.

The vice squad guys tell me to get out of town for a few weeks. Sharon and I have saved a bunch of money and want to get out of here anyway. We decide to head to Tahoe. We pack our bags and leave the next day.

I can't believe how self-destructive I was. I just wanted to die until that day we left LA. I remember feeling like I took down Goliath. I promised myself I would make something out of my life. I felt I had something to prove.

Chapter Nine

Eighteen Going on Thirty

When I moved out of my dad's house and in with Sharon, I took over the payments on my brother's 240Z. The Datsun is candy-apple red with a thick, white stripe from front to back. The car is supercharged with a beautiful hood scoop, an air dam on the front, and a spoiler on the back. The license plate reads STYLINZ.

Sharon and I take the 395 north to avoid interstate traffic. I love driving on remote highways. It's a beautiful day and hardly anyone is on the road. I put the pedal to the metal, and we are in Tahoe before we know it.

I love Tahoe! I have never lived in the mountains. It is so picturesque, and the smell of pine permeates the air. We passed many lovely, expansive ranches while driving here. One day, I hope to own a ranch with some horses.

When we go to the casinos, we don't get carded. It's great! I can't lose at the bar poker machines. A hundred bucks gives me eight hundred bucks return on my investment! There's a few guys at the bar who look up and congratulate me.

I say to the bartender, "Free drinks all the way around." I hand him a hundred bucks. "Keep the change!" I ordered a Chivas Rigal on the rocks.

I feel like a high roller! I take my winnings to a nearby blackjack table. Sharon roots me on. I am on a winning streak. We order another free drink and are feeling no pain. Everyone gathers around and watches me win almost every hand.

I decide to rent a limo to go to the discotheque for a little partying and dancing. Some good-looking guys at the blackjack table overhear us and ask if they can tag along.

I say, "Yeah, we'll see you there! We are going shopping!"

I spot a lady's clothing store by the exit and look at Sharon all giddy. "Let's get some sexy outfits!" I tell the valet to let the driver know we will be out in a few minutes. I find a beautiful silk white blouse with pastel pink and purple swirling patterns, and ruffles on the sleeves. It ties around my waist and shows off my sexy figure. I also find hip-hugger bellbottom pants with laces that tie up the front and the back. I look so sexy in my new outfit. Sharon finds a sleek black and silver jumpsuit. We look like runway models when we pose in the mirror together.

"Let's party!" I shout.

We head to the limo and duck into the plush interior. I feel like a high roller. A bottle of champagne sits in an ice bucket with two crystal glasses next to it. I pop the cork and it ricochets off the roof of the limo.

I hold up the bottle and shout, "Let the good times roll!"

Sharon grabs a glass, and I pour her some bubbly. We toast to our new life of glitz and glam! Before we know it, the limo pulls up to the club. The guys from the casino are waiting for us outside.

We waltz into the disco, lights flashing and music pulsating. It's packed and I wonder if we'll be able to get a table. When we approach the hostess, she says, "Tommy, your table is ready." Apparently, he is a regular here. We are escorted to a lovely, private round booth in the corner where we can talk without hearing the blaring music. Tommy immediately orders a bottle of champagne. He is tall, handsome, tanned, and has sandy-blond hair. He has a sweet smile and is quite charming.

When we settle in, I say, "So, Tommy, what do you do?"

"I manage Lakeview Resort, a timeshare resort on the lake. In fact, I'm looking for some salesgirls who can close deals. Do you know any?" He smiles, egging us on.

I say, "You found your gals," even though I have no idea if I can sell timeshares. But I'm on such a hot streak, I figure I can. And hopefully my Midas touch will rub off on Sharon.

"Stop by tomorrow and we'll see if there's a fit."

I'm super excited about the prospect of a real job with excellent earning potential. In contrast to the soul-deadening work I've done to survive, this is the real deal. I'm going to ace the interview.

We meet with Tommy the next day and, within half an hour, we're both offered jobs! It's great that we don't need real-estate licenses to sell timeshares. I discover I have such a knack for selling, I could sell ice to Eskimos. After just a few months of learning the craft, I am the number one salesperson at the club. For the first time ever, I have a sense of pride.

Unfortunately, Sharon isn't doing well selling timeshares. She doesn't have the golden touch like me. Plus, she misses her family in South Bend, Indiana. She is going home to California to put our stuff in storage, and then she'll go visit her family. I don't blame her, really. I could care less if I ever see my stepmom again, even though I do miss my siblings. But I am not going anywhere. I met a gorgeous baccarat dealer at Harrah's named Roy Murphy from New Jersey. *The fact that he's Irish sweetens the deal, and it doesn't hurt that he's easy on the eyes, if you know what I mean.* We are inseparable. I love visiting him at work. His tuxedo hugs his muscular body in all the right places. His stunning green eyes melt my heart. He has me wrapped around his finger. I don't mind, though. He smiles at me from across the room and tilts his head to say, come over here. He makes me feel like I'm the only person in the room. I don't hesitate.

For the first time in my life, I have a real boyfriend who makes me feel special, so I ask him to move in. He may as well; he's at my place every night after work. Bonus: he saves money on rent! I don't have to pay rent because I have a free condo at the resort. I am their top salesperson, after all. The condo sits right on the lake and is fully furnished with everything except my toothbrush and clothes. It's great living at the resort. I walk out my door, take a few steps, and I'm at the sales office.

Potential customers listen to our presentation in exchange for a free night at the resort. It's easy to sell timeshares, as it's cheaper for them to own a week in a condo at a timeshare resort, as oppose to staying in a hotel room where you have to go out to eat. I can't believe closing is so effortless. The gorgeous resort sells itself.

Roy usually gets home from work around 2:00 a.m. When he climbs into bed, we make mad, passionate love. He wakes me up from a deep sleep, but I don't mind. Waking up in his arms is a dream come true. It's great to finally enjoy making love rather than going through the motions while being checked out.

He often says, "I can't live without you. You drive me crazy."

He drives me crazy, too, in a good way. I can't get enough of him. He has seen the other side of life. He doesn't blink an eye when I tell him what I have been through. I am an open book. I don't care what anyone thinks about me. I am searching for real love.

Roy is a cokehead, which I guess is normal in the industry. I don't mind him using, but lately I've been noticing cash missing from my purse. I dismiss it at first. After all, we are a couple in love. He wouldn't steal from me, would he?

Roy got promoted at Harrah! He is a pit boss. He's working later and later every night. One morning, I wake up at 6:00 a.m. and wonder where he is. I get up, slip into a silky red robe, and head to the kitchen to brew some coffee. He is sitting on the couch with a mirror on the coffee table with a few lines of cocaine on it.

Seeing him doing coke reminds me of my missing cash. Maybe he's stealing money for drugs. "Hey, did you take money from my purse?"

"No. Why?"

"Well, I noticed $200 was missing. You're the only one around here besides me. Who else would it be?"

"You're just being paranoid." He waves me away and snorts his lines. He doesn't offer me any. Not that I'm interested, but still.

Even though we've been together for six months, I will not stay with a man who steals from me and lies about it. I promised myself that I won't let anyone use and abuse me again. It breaks my heart to realize there is nothing left, when the beginning was so wonderful. But that's life, I suppose. Why do things always have to end this way? I tell him it didn't have to end like this and to get his stuff and get out of here.

I am not going to lose my way again. There must be something better out there. I am worth more than this. One thing's for sure: I will certainly not find Mr. Right while staying with Mr. Wrong. Even though I'm excelling at the resort, it's time to spread my wings and fly. With my track record, any timeshare resort will hire me. And I'd like to go somewhere warm with a beach. I hate the cold. I open the latest *Timeshare News* and see that a Holiday Inn is converting their rooms to timeshare units in the Florida Keys at Mile Marker 80 in Isla Mirada. Maybe Sharon will go with me. I call her dad's house in South Bend and she answers the phone.

"Hey girl, what's up?"

"Nothing, I'm bored to death in sleepy hollow."

"Do you want to go to the Florida Keys with me? I'm going to get another timeshare job down there."

"Heck, yeah! I want out of my family's restaurant business. I am sick of waiting tables."

"How about I fly to South Bend and then we can drive your car to Florida?"

"You've got a deal!"

I call the resort in Florida to tell them I'm interested and share my stellar track record. They ask if they can contact Tommy for a reference. I say, "Of course."

Tommy knows I ended things with Roy and that I'm ready to get out of here. He gives them a great reference.

A girl named Michelle has been staying with me since I kicked Roy out. We met at the Lakeside Bar and Grill. I invited her to move in when I learned her boyfriend was beating her up. I think she's trustworthy, but I don't really know much about her. She doesn't have a car, so I let her take mine to the store while I am at work. I give her some money for groceries. It's great coming home to dinner made and the place clean.

I give my notice to Tommy and book a flight to South Bend out of San Francisco.

Michelle and I jump into my 240Z and zip to San Francisco where my brother lives. The plan is for her to meet my brother Paul at a restaurant after she drops me off at the airport. He is going to take over the car payments, as the loan is still in his name from when I bought it from him. She won't let me down after everything I have done for her — right?

Paul waited for her for two hours. I call him a few days later. I tell him to call the police to report the car missing.

I realize I can't trust anyone. I was so good to her and she stole my car. I no longer think I can trust anyone, maybe not even Sharon.

Watching my life unfold in front of me, I can see why I struggle so much with trusting people. I have to let go of the past and live in the moment. Please God, show me how!

Chapter Ten

Twenty-Three Going on Thirty-Five

Sharon and I start our jobs at the timeshare resort in the Florida Keys. I told them we were a package deal. But they put her to work in marketing because of her bleak track record in sales. Her job is to hand out invitations or "Passports to Paradise" to all the tourist attractions. It looks like an American passport and has coupons for two-for-one dinners at Johnny's, the seafood restaurant on the island, as well as other establishments offering tourist attractions. Tourists also get one night at the resort for listening to a sales presentation.

It's not long before I'm giving the group presentations. I've always loved the feeling of all eyes on me. I stand on a platform in a big conference room where families sit with a salesperson at small round tables. I walk them through what they are doing now — staying at a hotel, or what they could be doing — owning a week in a condo. After the presentation, the salespeople walk each couple through what I just presented. I mill about and introduce myself, asking if they have any questions. I am so good at overcoming objections; I can do it in my sleep. After dealing with the customer's objections, I go for the close.

I am on fire in the sales department and closing our salespeople's deals. My nickname is "The Closer."

I love the hot and humid weather here. It's great to be back at the beach. I am getting plenty of Vitamin D, looking and feeling alive again. I wear sexy sun dresses and high-heeled sandals. Every day after work Sharon and I go to the resort bar and order a rum-runner cocktail or two and watch the sunset over the ocean. We wear our bikinis under our dresses. I slip off my dress, leave it on the bar and jump in the pool. It's great meeting all kinds of fun people from places near and far. We have access to the resort's boats and sign for our meals whenever we want. It feels good to be on top of my game again.

One night, a cute guy from the bar turns on his bar stool and smiles at me when I jump in the pool. He sips his cocktail with a shit-eating grin.

I swim up to the side of the pool. "What are you looking at?"

He says, "A beautiful lady."

I laugh. "Why don't you join me?"

He says, "That's an offer I can't refuse," and dives into the pool. He swims under water toward me and puts his hands around my skinny waist. Chills run down my spine.

"I'm Jackie. And you are?"

"Prince Charming, but you can call me Josh."

We get out of the pool and sit by the bar and talk for a bit. His parents have a second home in Key Largo, a few miles away. Given that those homes cost a pretty penny, they are obviously well-to-do. He is visiting from St. Louis for a few days. We get together every night before he leaves. I really like him and want to get to know him better; in fact, I wish he lived here. Josh is short and stocky with a great body. He has a strong, confident, personality; he is playful and somewhat cocky and arrogant. He repeatedly asks me to move to St. Louis. I'm tempted but not yet convinced it's the right move.

Sharon married a great guy she met at the pool bar shortly after we arrived. They had an informal wedding on the beach in front of his rented cottage. Sharon and her husband Bobbie live next to the resort. She didn't make it in the timeshare business, so she took a job as a hostess at a nearby high-end Chinese restaurant. The problem is: she drinks too much, can't get out of bed in the morning, and is obsessed with guys and sex.

Sharon and I hardly talk anymore. One day she calls me after work. "I have to tell you something."

"Okay, shoot."

"Can you come over?"

"Sure."

I walk to her house next door. She offers me a wine cooler.

"Promise you won't judge me?"

"Promise."

"I've been having an affair with my boss. He's married, too, but he plans to leave his wife. I really love him."

"Don't mess up a good thing, Sharon."

"I told you not to judge."

"Seriously, guys like Bobbie don't come around that often. Trust me on this one."

Her husband is a good looking blond-haired, blue-eyed guy who has a steady job in construction. I like Bobbie.

"Bobbie is never going to amount to anything. He's a handyman. I need someone who can take care of me, so I don't have to work."

"Why don't you want to work?"

She ignores my question. "So, here's the other thing."

"There's more?"

"Well, yeah. I'm pregnant and I think it's my boss's baby."

"Oh, geez. Have you told your boss?"

"No, I don't know if it's his. He's Chinese. I'm worried, as Bobbie is going to be with me in the delivery room. If the baby comes out with black hair and squinty eyes, he's going to know it's not his. I don't know what to do."

"I can't help you there. I can't believe you've gotten yourself into this mess. I'm sorry. I have to go." I don't have time for people like her in my life.

* * *

A few weeks later, I get a call from Bobbie asking me if I know where Sharon is. He says he came home to an empty house. I tell him the truth. I don't know where she is.

Months later, Sharon calls to tell me she moved to Torrance, California. She had a little blonde baby girl. I congratulate her while thinking, *Oh great, she left her husband for nothing. I have had it with her using and abusing people.*

I miss Josh terribly. We've been having a long-distance love affair since he went home to St. Louis. He's been urging me to move there, so I decide to go for it. I give my notice at work. I'm not sure it's the right thing for me, but I really like him and don't want to lose him.

A few weeks later, I pack up my clothes and move to St. Louis. Josh lives in a high-end townhome in the suburbs. I don't have a car, but thankfully he has two, so I drive his Ford Bronco, while he drives his Pantera sports car to and from work. He owns a restaurant called Pantera's Pizza.

Josh has impeccable taste and deep pockets. His place is gorgeous. But I don't like that he is such a neat freak. He even alphabetizes his canned goods! He drives me crazy. It's moving into fall here. I like to see the trees changing colors, but's it's been cold and rainy in St. Louis. I don't have the proper wardrobe for this climate, so after a big fight about how everything must be perfect around here, he takes me to buy a whole new wardrobe.

I love the fine dining and incredible jazz scene in St. Louis. Josh is in the restaurant business, so we're treated like VIPs. His father is also in the industry, having made a fortune in the restaurant-equipment business. As a hobby his dad breeds thoroughbred horses for horse racing. It's racing season, so we are going to Arlington Park Racetrack near Chicago to watch their horses race every few weeks. I love being around the horses and wonder if I'll ever have my own. It is exciting to be a part of the horse-racing scene.

Josh knows everything about me. Maybe too much. I told him about my past, but now wish I hadn't. I wait on him hand and foot. We have great sex, but something is missing. I can sense he will never commit to me. He's a player and flirts with pretty girls right in front of me. I have mentioned the M-word a few times, but he always changes the subject. I think his parents object, too, and want him to marry a socialite from St. Louis. His mom introduces him to her friend's daughters when we are at his parent's house for big parties. She has a smug look, like they're better than I am. It makes me angry and tempts me to leave Josh. He won't do anything to piss off the money tree.

I feel so empty and alone. Josh doesn't want me to work and won't let me out of his sight. My main activity is going to the gym every day. Afterward, I prepare a lovely dinner for him. I learned from Mom how to be a great cook. Despite my catering to his every whim, he comes home later and later every night. Some nights, I let his dinner get cold and go to bed before he gets home. I'm tired of waiting for him.

The manager of the gym urges me to come to work for her. She says, "You may as well get paid; you're here every day."

She's right. I have memorized all the aerobics classes. I do about three, sometimes four, a day to blow off steam and to ease my boredom. It is an all-women's gym. Josh won't have it any other way.

Finally, when I've had enough, I tell Josh, I'm going to be an aerobics instructor at my gym. He tells me I can do whatever I want. Yeah, right. He is such a control freak.

It's 1982, the height of the aerobics craze. I've learned a lot about the business and am a great aerobics instructor. I enjoy making my own money. It's a respectable living. I am 20, but I feel 35. I wish Josh would grow up.

He opened a night club called *Flashback* recently and comes home even later every night than he did at the restaurant. He promised me he would be home by eight tonight. It's nine and he hasn't even called me to tell me when he's coming home. I'm pissed, but I am not going to call him. I eat without him and then throw his dinner in the trash. I leave a note under a plate cover I use to keep his meals warm. The note reads, *I am tired of waiting for you, in more ways than one.*

I go to sleep, realizing he is never going to marry me. Even though I want to marry him, I must accept he won't marry a girl with my background. It makes me feel like I am not good enough. It hurts.

He came home at 2:30 a.m. I lay here pretending to sleep. I get up early. I didn't sleep much, but I have to go to work. Josh doesn't even bother to wake up to talk to me about my note. I'm going to swallow my pride, pack my bags while he's at work tonight, and move in with a girl I work with at the gym. Jeanette and I have become good friends. She knows all about how Josh has been treating me. She has told me more than once; I can stay with her if I want to leave him. I see Jeanette in the breakroom when I get to work. She looks at me and says, "You look awful girl. Are you feeling ok?" I break down and start crying.

"I didn't sleep last night. I've had it with Josh. Did you mean what you've said about me staying with you?"

"Yes, of course. I'm happy you're not going to take his shit anymore."

"Can we go get my stuff from his place after work? He won't be there. He'll be at the restaurant and then go to the club."

"For sure. I'm here for you, girl. Don't worry. Everything going to be o.k."

"Thanks, Jeanette. I really appreciate it."

"Why don't I do your 9 o'clock class. You can do my 10 if you want or I can do it if you're not feeling up for it."

"Are you sure? I can do your 10 o'clock. I just need a little time to eat some breakfast and drink some coffee."

"I got you, girl. I'll go tell the manager we're going to switch classes."

"You're the best! I'm taking you out for dinner tonight after we get my stuff."

"Sounds good. We can order some Chinese food, and have it delivered to my place when we get home." she says, as she heads out the door of the breakroom.

On our way to Josh's place after work, Jeanette tells me she that she spoke to our manager and told her I was moving in with her.

She says with a big grin on her face, "She's going make our schedules the same, so we can drive to work together!"

"You're an angel. I don't know what I would do without ya."

Thankfully, Josh's car isn't here so we go inside and pack up my stuff in no time flat. We managed to get all my toiletries and shoes in my suitcases and take my clothes and coats out on the hangers. I left the gray fox coat Josh got me for Christmas. *I cannot be bought anymore. He can have his damn money and his life back.*

It's late December; next week is New Year's Eve. I'm sad that I won't be spending it with Josh, but happy I am going into the New Year standing up for myself and not allowing him to treat me like he has the past few months. He left a message for me this morning at work. I waited to call him back until after he went to the restaurant. I left a message for him on his answering machine.

I said, "I am sorry, I moved out without talking to you. You are always so busy now with the restaurant and night club. I am tired of waiting for you night after night.

I moved in with a girlfriend from work. I need some time to think about what I want to do with the rest of life. I may go visit my family in California. Please don't call me.

* * *

The past few months have flown by. I feel good about my decision to move out of Josh's place, but I do miss him. He has called me once or twice to make small talk. I think he's giving me my space, yet hoping I tell him I want him back. I am not going to make the first move. If he wants me in his life for good, he's going to have to make the first move.

It's Valentine's Day, and Josh asks me out for dinner. I say yes, thinking he has a surprise for me. He shows up in a limo and says we are going to my favorite restaurant, Tony's. I just know he is going to ask me to marry him. After our romantic dinner, we go to his house and make mad, passionate love. But the proposal never comes. I am heartbroken.

He leaves early in the morning for work while I am sleeping. I wake up feeling empty and confused. I decide I'm finished with him. I call a taxi to take me home. I call Daniel in LA. He says I can live with him. I can't wait to get to know him. I didn't get the chance to growing up because of the 12 years between us. I was only eight when he went to Vietnam. When he returned from the war, he got his own place in Long Beach. I give my notice at work and let Jeanette know I moving to Long Beach to live with my brother.

It's time for me to get on with my life. It's obvious Josh is never going to commit to me. I am over him!

* * *

It is great to be near my older siblings again. Laurie is married and lives in the Angeles Crest Mountains, about an hour away. Patty and Paul are living in West Hollywood together. It's the first time we all live near each other and can go out clubbing together. I love it! The night clubs are hot in LA.

I got a job as a waitress. I have no skills other than teaching aerobics, and there is no money in that. Unfortunately, I can't use my timeshare-sales skills. The laws have changed, and I need my real-estate license to sell resort timeshare units in California. I really want to get my license, but I must make some make money first if I am going to get my own place. I work morning, noon, and night waiting tables and making great tips! It's hard work, but worth it.

I've been in LA almost a year now. Patty, Paul and I — all single — are going out tonight. It's Valentine's Day, so we call ourselves the Lonely Hearts' Club. Maybe we will meet a special someone; you never know. We are going to Popcorns, a night club with a discotheque in Marina Del Rey. They are throwing a pajama party. I am game for dressing up, even though Patty and Paul aren't. They are going to root me on. I'm in the red nightie with matching red robe I got last year, the night I thought Josh would propose; the night I went to bed an unengaged woman. Thinking about last year is making my blood boil. I am drinking way too much, but need a little liquid courage before I get up on that stage.

It's time for the costume judging. I am nervous about getting on the stage, but what the heck! I strut my stuff across the stage, shoulders back and hips forward like a runway model, dancing to the music. I parade back and forth, working the audience. I'm feeling tipsy.

I didn't win the contest, but I think I win something even better — someone's heart. I notice a stranger smiling at me while I was dancing on the stage. I tell my brother and sister about him. They glance over at him and he is looking right at us, so I approach him.

He has a buff body like a body builder, and blond hair. He's looking intensely at me with beautiful green eyes.

"I'm Jackie. Who are you?"

"I'm Borge. You sure looked good up there. I think you should have won the contest."

His accent is so sexy, it melts my heart. "Where are you from? I love your accent."

"Sweden. I'm living with a family here in exchange for some finished carpentry work. I've had some other great side jobs here, too. I did some work for Madonna in her home recording studio."

"Wow! You must be talented. Either that or you have some good connections." I laugh and he joins in. "So, did you get to meet Madonna?"

"I'll never tell."

"Maybe one day, I'll get it out of you," I say, hoping it's true.

He is so charming, and his smile melts my heart. It's love at first sight. We are inseparable. Unfortunately, his visa will expire soon, and he must go back to Sweden to renew it. He really wants me to go with him, but we don't have enough money for me to go. I must have a round-trip airfare ticket in order to get a tourist visa for more than 30 days. I tell him I will go in June after I save some money.

* * *

Two months fly by. I can't believe he is leaving tomorrow, but not before my birthday dinner on April 18. I am 23 years old. We have the most romantic dinner with red wine and delicious steak. He brings up the M-word.

He says, "Jackie, how do you feel about marriage?"

"Marriage in general or marrying you?"

He laughs. "Well, if we get married in Sweden, I can come back to LA for good."

I say, "Let's see what the future holds."

I am so excited! Borge wants to marry me!! Spring always makes me feel like new beginnings are on the horizon. I am so glad I broke free of St. Louis and came to LA. Maybe it is destiny, but I still want to take it one step at a time. He is going back to Sweden tomorrow. I don't want to leave LA, but I'm not going to let him slip through my fingers.

I am working from 6:00 a.m. for the breakfast shift through the lunch shift until 3:00 p.m. at this diner near my house. I have just enough time to go home and rest before I go to an expensive seafood restaurant near the beach and serve dinner until 10:00 p.m. and then drinks until 2:00 a.m., when the bar closes. I am exhausted, but it's for a worthy cause.

* * *

It's been two months since I have seen Borge. I am so excited that I am going to Sweden to see him in a few days. I won't have to work this brutal schedule anymore. I saved nearly $10,000! I am nervous to go to a foreign county where I don't speak the language. He claims all the kids our age speaks perfect English, so not to worry.

I don't know what to expect. I just know I love this man and he loves me. We're going to get married!

I arrive in Sweden after a 13-hour flight and a layover in Copenhagen. Borge asked me to bring alcohol for his friends and family, so I crammed my luggage with booze. I can't believe I make it through customs. I was afraid they would bust me, but they don't even check my bags.

I see Borge waiting for me with open arms on other side of customs. I smile and wave. I can't wait to start my new life here! We live with his folks. I don't mind, because they are the kindest people. His mother loves having a helper in the kitchen. I am happy to help. She doesn't speak as much English as his father, but we talk with our hearts. It feels good to be part of a family again.

Borge's mom shows me how to make a smörgåstårta — or sandwich cake, a popular Swedish dish. First you take bread and cut the bread crust to make perfect squares. Then you mix ricotta cheese with ketchup and relish. You lay out the squares of bread next to each other to make a rectangle on a pan. You spread the cheese filling on each piece and then you put another piece of bread on top and repeat until you have three layers. You spread the rest of the filling on top and on the sides like a cake. Then you decorate the top with shrimp, sliced cucumber and fresh dill from the garden. It is so beautiful. We are planning to meet Borge's friends, Anders and Matts, for lunch, where I will share the smörgåstårta.

He was right about the kids our age speaking perfect English. I give Anders a bottle of Cuervo Gold Tequila and Matts a bottle of Jack Daniels. I can tell by their big smiles that they really appreciate it. Alcohol is very expensive here. I cut the sandwich cake for them and we crack open the bottle of Jack Daniels. Everyone is so nice to me. They love the smörgåstårta. We are going camping tomorrow to spend the Midsummer Festival weekend with his friends.

We set off for the festival early in the morning, as it's going to take a few hours to get there. Everything is so green and there are lakes everywhere. We drive through small country towns that look like postcards. We stop to pick up some treats at a market. There are more bicycles in the parking lot than there are cars — so different from home! I am excited to be in a foreign country. My senses have come alive. Listening to people speaking Swedish, including Borge and his friends, is so fascinating. I can't wait to learn to speak the language. The smell of the bread in the bakery makes me hungry, as do the many different types of cheese and cold cuts. I order a little bit of everything. We plan to eat sandwiches on the way.

Our campground is on a lake with tents pitched everywhere. I notice it's mostly kids our age. We pitch our tent and unload the car. I am a little nervous. Everyone is speaking Swedish, and I don't understand a word. Borge introduces me to more of his friends. As soon as they learn I am American, they gather around and ask me tons of questions in perfect English. I feel like a celebrity.

As the night wears on, Borge and his friends are drinking heavily. I don't like to drink too much and don't want to get drunk. It's getting dark and chilly, so we build a big open fire near the lake. I can't believe how wasted everyone is. They drink right from the bottle and pass it around to everyone sitting by the fire. I'm going back to our tent to write in my journal. I tell Borge I am exhausted and going to bed.

He says, "I'll be there in a little while."

I fall asleep with a pen in my hand. Jetlag has gotten the best of me.

I start my Swedish-language class in the fall after a lovely summer here. It's great meeting people from all over the world. I really like my Lebanese classmates, who have big hearts and like to eat good food. We often meet for lunch at a café next to the school. One day, an American from Chicago is playing the piano and singing great old jazz standards. She overhears me speaking English with my friends from school. In between songs, she introduces herself as Desiree. She has a milky-white complexion with a natural glow and jet-black hair that she wears short in a mullet. She's playful, intelligent and witty, but most of all she's real. Unlike most women jazz performers who woo the crowds with their sexy, sequined gowns, Desiree wears a classic tuxedo and woos the audience with her sultry voice and show-stopping smile. When I walk into the café, it feels as if I am reunited with a long-lost friend. I am an American in a foreign land and didn't realize until now how much I miss my fellow countrymen.

We have an instant connection. She really gets me. There's no pretense here. We become the best of friends. I go to the café every day to watch her perform and to hang out with her between sets. We are inseparable. She is going back to the States soon, unless she can find more work here. I ask Borge if he knows any clubs or hotels that might be looking for a jazz artist. He tells me he will ask his friend's father, who manages the Grand Hotel. Happily, he finds her a job on the coast. Desiree signs a year contract at one of the Grand Hotels in Gothenburg, Sweden. There's a ferry there that goes to Hamburg,

Germany. Borge and I are going to drive there to look for a Mercedes after we drop off Desiree. Borge drives a Porsche, but it's only a two-seater and repairs cost a fortune. He's hoping to trade it in for a Mercedes. Borge and I take Desiree to the hotel so she can meet her new employer and colleagues. They give her a room at the hotel and a salary to perform in the hotel night club. We take her through the ins and outs of the transportation system — primarily trains. She loves it here and I understand why. I've missed the ocean.

Borge officially asks me to marry him on the ferry over to Germany. I can tell he is a little nervous. He stutters, "Have you had enough time to decide if we should get married?"

I am caught off-guard. "Yeah, I think so."

"Well … do you want to marry me?"

I am still a little hesitant. I don't know why, because I do love him, I think. I really don't know what love is. I thought I loved Roy, but now I know I just liked feeling special.

"Yes, I do, but can we wait until next year? I really want to learn Swedish first."

He smiles real big. "Okay, I can't wait to tell my parents."

His parents are delighted for us. We plan to marry next September in a 600-year-old church in his little town of Kumla. It's November now.

Swedish comes easily to me. I think listening to my mother and father speak French helped me develop an ear for languages. I've learned enough in the Swedish language class to communicate and get around. It's winter here and frigid. I sometimes need to wear snowshoes to cross the field between his house and the street to catch the bus to school . I found a gym in town that wants me to teach aerobics in the spring. They need a few months to get a room ready for me, and I can't wait. With spring around the corner, I can start riding Borge's mom's bike to school, rather than taking the bus.

* * *

Spring arrives and, as an American aerobics' instructor, I am the talk of town. My classes are packed with young Swedish girls. I assume it is because I am a great instructor. Little do I know it is really because they want to practice their English. I don't care. I am having the time of my life getting to know everything about this culture. I enjoy Swedes' pleasant and inquisitive nature.

The one thing I don't like is they drink too much-or at least Borge and his buddies do. They hang out and drink as often as they can. I don't like to go with them every time and figure guys need their alone time. When he's too drunk to drive, he spends the night at his friend's place. One time I got a call from the police asking me to pick him up in the morning at the station. They found him in a bar parking lot, passed out in his car.

With the weather warming up here, we are going to his parent's property in Lapland. His father is Lapp, which is similar to the Eskimos in Alaska. He is small in stature with squinty eyes. Lapp country is referred to as the land of the midnight sun, where the sun doesn't set until 10 p.m. They have a teepee set up on the land where we will stay. We pack and head north in his father's Volvo station wagon. It takes us all day to get here. It's beautiful country. There are hardly any homes here and only a few places to shop. We stop to get provisions at a trading post where there are many Lapp people trading furs and dried meats. Borge's father's family used to follow the reindeer and hunt them for their pelts and meat. We see a trading post and stop to get some lunch. They have fresh goat's milk cheese and smoked reindeer meat which I haven't had before. It's delicious. I am scarfing it down as it's so good. I didn't realize how hungry I was.

It's much colder here than in Kumla. We arrive at the teepee late in the evening. It's real dark outside, as there are no streetlights here in the country. I can't see the surroundings. We are tired so we set up our sleeping bags in the teepee and fall asleep. It's hard to sleep with the owls hooting and the deer grunting and bleating. Borge says it's their mating calls.

We are up at the crack of dawn, loading the canoe on top of the Volvo. The plan is to head to a nearby lake and go fishing. Everything is so green and there are lakes everywhere. When we arrive, we put the canoe in the water, and then our fishing lines. The fish bite as soon as we drop the poles in the water. Once we've caught a dozen or more fish, we head back to the teepee to smoke them. His father is so proud of us. He hangs the fish from a post at the top of the teepee. He builds a fire in the center of it, so the fish will smoke over the fire. There is a hole in the top of the teepee to let out the smoke.

We sit outside by a river to eat our lunch of smoked meat and cheese and sip some wine. I love it here, but I don't know how his dad endured the winters. There is a little chill in the air, so we head back to the teepee to warm up. We discuss wedding plans. It will be a small wedding with his family and a few friends. My family is going to celebrate with us when we return to the States. We will head back to LA a week after the wedding.

Today is the big day. I am dressed in a beautiful white velvet three-quarter-length dress with lace like Madonna wore in the *Like a Virgin* video. I wish I was a virgin. My dress is shorter in the front and longer in the back, and I am wearing a veil. My Irish Catholic relatives would approve. I feel like a princess, getting married in this gorgeous, ancient church. Around 50 friends and his family members are here. I am so nervous. I hope I don't forget how to say my vows in Swedish.

As I walk down the aisle, I'm thinking, *What am I doing? Why am I doing this? Is it because I am the only girl in my family not married, or is it because I want to spend the rest of my life with Borge?* I can't believe I'm having these thoughts. Perhaps it's normal to have reservations when you're making a commitment for life. I try to push my doubts aside, but the uneasiness remains. I hope Borge doesn't notice. I don't think he does; he has been drinking all day and is a little tipsy. When we stand face to face, I smile but it feels forced, like a painted-on smile. I wish my family were here; maybe then I would feel better. I can't wait to see them when we get back to the States.

Wow! Seeing my wedding to Borge after all these years brings back memories of the hope I had for our future. I was so young and didn't know what love really was. I realize now I should have listened to that small, still voice inside of me.

Chapter Eleven

Twenty-Five Going on Forty

It's great to be back in LA, everything is falling right into place. Borge and I found a little two-bedroom house on Sepulveda Boulevard to rent. I got a job as a leasing agent with a developer who builds apartment complexes. He says if I can sell timeshares, I can rent units. Borge found a job working for a building contractor, framing houses. We spend our weekends having fun with my family barbequing or going to hot spots around the city for Sunday Brunch. I love LA!

Lord, thank you for giving me the courage to get my life back on track. I couldn't have done it without you.

I wish Borge believed in God. Whenever I bring up how much God has blessed us, he says, "We have blessed ourselves." He's an atheist, like my father. Even more troubling than his lack of spiritual beliefs are his alcoholic tendencies. I thought he drank a lot in Sweden, but he is drinking even more here. Almost every day, he pops open a beer after work and drinks until he goes to bed. He is a happy drunk, but it is hardly any consolation. Anytime we have plans to go out, he starts drinking early and then passes out before we leave. I'm sick of making excuses for him. After a few months in LA, he stops going to my brothers' and sisters' houses altogether. He prefers to stay home and drink. He's so checked out. Maybe he's drinking because he misses his friends and family. I ask him what's wrong and, slurring his words, he says he just wants to stay home and rest after a long week of working.

Thankfully, I have my family to cheer me up.

I miss my American girlfriend from Sweden. I am going to call her to catch up. I call the Grand Hotel is Sweden and was told she doesn't work there anymore. *I'm going to try the number I have for her in Chicago.* Desiree's mom answers the phone and tells me Desiree is in Japan performing now. She says she will give her my number the next time she calls her.

It's Saturday and I am knee-deep in laundry and cleaning while Borge is on the couch watching soccer and drinking beer. I can't believe we've been married for almost a year and this is my new life. It sucks. I hear the phone ringing while I'm trying to get in the house with a hamper full of clean clothes. I throw it on the floor and grab the phone.

I hear my sweet friend Desiree on the other end of the phone.

"Hey girl, how's married life?"

"It's awful! One of the biggest mistakes of my life."

"Oh girl, I'm sorry. My agent in Chicago found me work in Japan. I like it here, but I miss ya. My promoter in Japan has so many American artists working for him that he can't focus on just me. He can pay you to manage me, if you can find me more work."

"Sweet! What's your number? I will give you a call in a few days. I need a plan."

The work week flies by, we are so busy at the office. Borge and I are celebrating our first wedding anniversary tonight. It's Saturday, I have a 2 o'clock appointment to get my hair cut and colored. I am excited about going out for a change, plus I love dressing up. I found a really pretty black cocktail dress. Our reservation is at 6. It's 5:30 when I walk in the door. He is passed out on the couch. I try to wake him, but he rolls over with his back facing me now. I take the whisky bottle on the coffee table and pour a stiff drink, sit down and plot my exit. I am so fed up with doing all the cooking, cleaning, grocery shopping, and laundry - while he sits around and drinks.

I woke up before him and make coffee. He is still asleep on the couch.

He wakes up and says, "Is that coffee I smell?"

I say, "I don't want to live like this anymore. I want a divorce."

The next words out of his mouth take my breath away.

"Can we stay married for one more year, so I can get my permanent residency?"

I can't believe he is asking me that. I want out of here. "Sure, I don't plan on marrying anytime soon, but I am moving to Japan."

I'm really hurt that he doesn't even try to get me to stay. He just wants his Green Card.

I understand why he married me now. Perhaps that is how my stepmom felt when my dad left to live on his sailboat two hours away and she was responsible for taking care of us. I feel used and not worth fighting for. I am out of here!

I walk into the bedroom and pack my clothes. While he is in the shower, I pack my car and check into a weekly rental. I call Desiree and tell her I am going to give my notice at work. I am so excited to see her. We had a blast in Sweden.

A few weeks later, I am on a flight heading to Japan. I see her in the distance after I cleared customs. She has a sweet way of always making me feel good; I am so glad I left Borge.

"Welcome to Japan!" We embrace each other.

"Thanks, girl, for setting this up for me. It's good to be here." We head out to the curb with my luggage in tow. She hails a taxi.

Japan is so different from anything I have ever experienced. Desiree lives in Osaka, which feels so much more crowded than LA. People squeeze into subways and elevators where you can hardly move. The roads are filled with cars honking in bumper-to-bumper traffic. Americans are celebrities here. I am a beautiful blonde, turning heads wherever I go. The Japanese love jazz and there are more clubs in one square mile than in all of LA. Most are the size of a living room and housed in towering skyscrapers. There are neon light murals projected onto buildings with images like Superman and Mickey Mouse. It's thrilling to live in a faraway place so different from home. We eat and drink such exotic food and wine. My favorite food here is sushi and sake. We live in a little studio apartment with a Murphy bed, a bookshelf on one side, and a table on the other side of the built-in cabinet.

Desiree takes me to meet her promoter, Hiroshi. He is a little guy with a Napoleon complex. He acts like he is God's gift to women.

He says, "With your looks, you shouldn't have any problems opening doors for Desiree. I want you to go into the clubs when she is preforming and promote her to the clientele. Ask them if they know of any more clubs wanting an American jazz performer. "

I say, "It shouldn't be that difficult. I did it for her in Sweden. I can do it here."

American jazz artists attract Japanese clientele who flock to their performances. I am at the club tonight. There is a bigshot sitting in a booth in the corner, surrounded by several beautiful woman, none of whom look Japanese. Champagne is being popped left and right. I think I'll go introduce myself.

I am wearing one of Desiree's beaded dresses that shows off my slim figure. She has many gorgeous dresses she wears to perform here. In Sweden, she wore tuxedo-looking outfits, but she says in Japan they like you to dress to the nines.

I stroll over to the bigshot's booth and say, "How is everyone enjoying the show?"

He says, "She's great. Please join us."

I sit down. "Please allow me to introduce myself. I am Jackie, Desiree's manager. She is good. Isn't she?"

He glances at the other gals and says, "Ladies, please give me a few minutes to talk business with Jackie."

They smile, get up, and walk to the bar.

"I am Takigawa. I own the largest entertainment companies here. I would like Desiree to perform with Isao Suzuki, an upright bass player and jazz legend. I think she will compliment him by opening the show. We have a concert tour in a few months where I am investing over a million dollars in the production and could use your help."

I thought Hiroshi was full of himself, but Takigawa is taking it to a whole new level. He is quite sure of himself and very arrogant.

He says, "Do you want to discuss it more over dinner tonight?"

I am delighted. I can hardly contain myself.

"I would love to!"

He takes me to a lavish restaurant that serves incredible food, like delicious melt-in-your-mouth blowfish . They call it Fugu. He tells me that if the fish is not cooked correctly, it's poisonous. I say, "I hope the chef knows what he's doing. I don't want to get poisoned." I wait to let Takigawa take the first bite. He smiles and says, "Go ahead. It won't kill you. I take a bite. It melts in my mouth leaving a buttery, savory flavor.

After dinner, we end up at a hotel. He parks the car, walks to my side of the car, opens it up, and helps me out. I'm happy to see that chivalry isn't dead. I'm drunk from an evening of fine food and too much champagne.

We walk into the hotel. The front desk has no attendants. Instead, there is a large digital monitor for room selection. You scroll through images of the various available rooms. Takigawa chooses the room, inserts his credit card, and the key drops down. When we open the door to our room, there's a big round bed and a large Jacuzzi in the middle. As soon as we enter, he pushes me up against the wall and kisses me passionately. I am a little taken aback, as I haven't been with anyone since Borge. Just thinking about Borge makes my blood run cold, so I force him out of my mind and surrender to kissing Takigawa. I am exhausted from the flight. When he walks into the bathroom, I lie down on the bed and pass out. When I wake up, I'm in my bra and panties and my dress hangs over a chair. He turns on the Jacuzzi and pours bubble bath salt into the water. It looks so inviting. He slips off his undershirt and boxers and asks me to join him. I smile, stretch like a cat, get up, get undressed, and get in. He is so forceful and sure of himself as we make love.

A little guilt creeps in, but it's time for me to get on with my life. As far as I am concerned, I am not married anymore. Takigawa orders room service from the phone on the tub deck. I could get used to this treatment. We talk about the concert tour over breakfast. He is eager for me to get started helping him find dancers for the tour. I'm confident I can do a good job. After all, I have mastered the art of the deal.

On our way back to the apartment, he stops at a place with a huge variety of fur coats in a temperature-controlled vault. There are so many, my head is spinning. He urges me to try on ones that catch my eye.

Takigawa says, "Don't be shy. I want you to have your favorite one, as a gift from me."

I really like the London Fog style raincoat with chinchilla fur on the inside. He tells me it's reversible, but a beautiful full-length black sable mink coat catches my eye. I feel like a movie star in it. I'm blown away by his generosity. I wonder if he owns this place. He drives a Honda Accord, but he is obviously loaded. He drops me off at Desiree's and my apartment outside of Osaka in a suburb called Nakasu. It's enchanting here. Everything is so surreal. I've got a new lease on life, another page, another story. I can't wait to tell Desiree the good news. She is making green tea when I walk in sporting my new mink coat. She has the most beautiful smile. She says, "Wow! Look at you girl!!" I say, "We're going on a concert tour!! Hold on tight, girl. We're in for the ride of our lives."

Japan has bathhouses open all night, which Takigawa and I often frequent after drinking too much at the clubs. After the girls scrub you with bath salts, you sit in a steam room and sweat until you can't bear it anymore. Then you plunge into an ice bath that's very invigorating.

I fly back to LA to hire dancers and a choreographer for the show. Takigawa gave me $5,000 to get an apartment for us. I am having the time of my life! He is investing big money in the show, so everything must be perfect. I rent a condo in LA to meet with the prospective dancers. It is a way for him to have a presence in LA. He wants to get a foothold in the LA scene and tap into the entertainment industry here. He also wants me to recruit girls to work in his night clubs in Japan.

Japanese nightclubs are called hostess bars. A Japanese gal that looks like a geisha sits on the floor at a low table on colorful fine silk cushions and serves the gentlemen their cocktails. Her face is painted with white makeup and her eyes with dramatic black paint. She wears a black wig with a big bun and two chopsticks at an angle holding the bun in place. She's dressed in a traditional Japanese kimono. The geisha girls serve the customers exquisite, fine food that is so beautifully presented. It looks like a masterpiece on a plate.

American girls are called hostesses who sit and talk with the Japanese clientele. They like to speak English. Girls from Brazil and many other countries dance in the clubs. Takigawa has beautiful, young girls from all over the world working in his night clubs. Perhaps this inspired the name of his company, World Echo. I realize why he is willing to invest in Desiree. He owns hundreds of clubs. He knows I can set up shop in LA and recruit girls to work for him.

When I return to Japan, Takigawa tells me he wants to show me something. I'm excited. I wonder if it's a special surprise for me. He drives quickly through small alleys, swerving right and then left, while not saying much. I lose track of where we are. I can't put my finger on it, but something is up. The scene becomes more puzzling with each passing moment.

He takes me into a large warehouse in a back-alley where he has a production company. We walk into an office and he introduces me to his manager. My eyes are drawn to nine monitors over the manager's desk where they are filming girls in porn movies. *What is this place? Is Takigawa a porn producer?*

In another part of the warehouse, I am shocked by what I see: girls lying on grass mats on the floor. Most of them are Asian, and a few look Spanish, but they're probably Filipino. I'm horrified when I suspect these girls are being sold into slavery. My stomach is in knots and I feel like I might throw up. I want to run out of here and never look back. Little do these girls know they may never see their homes or families again. Takigawa says he wants me to get him American girls. I am so upset; *I can't believe he would stoop this low.*

I notice a girl shooting up. *They're probably all hooked on drugs. And guess who is supplying the drugs? Takigawa!* I remember him handing the manager a bag of white stuff when we came into the building. At the time, I couldn't make sense of it. Now, I'm guessing it is heroin. This guy is as low as they come. I want out of this deal, out of this warehouse, and out of his life.

How am I going to extract myself from this situation? I must convince him I'm willing to help. I feel incredibly anxious but must play it cool. This is where my sales training comes in handy. I put on an air of confidence as I plot my escape.

I say, "I have some ideas for you, but let's talk about it over dinner."

He buys it, or at least I think he does. Two guys in a high-end sportscar follow us to the restaurant. I've got a bad feeling. I don't want him to know I am not on board. He knows I know too much already.

I've heard of Americans getting thrown off tall buildings while the authorities claim suicide. I realize that the rumor I heard about him months ago is true: Takigawa is the head of the Japanese mafia. I didn't want to believe it at the time. Why did I not listen? I am in so deep that if I don't get out of here, I will probably never be seen again.

Even though I'm terrified, I must get a grip. He needs me to help him get American girls so he can corner the market here. I have leverage. If I can convince him that I am interested, I can return to LA and move out of his condo before he knows I am not coming back. I lie through my teeth, kicking into survival mode.

In the pouring rain, we walk into a little Japanese restaurant in a dark corner of the city. I tell him I need to use the restroom and to please order me a Chivas Regal on the rocks. As I sit on the toilet, panicking, I plot my escape. I wonder if I can fit through the small window in the bathroom. I squeeze through the window, then run for my life in the pouring rain to the nearest busy street.

I am soaking wet and freezing, jumping around to stay warm. Most of the cabs zip right past me like I'm invisible. *C'mon, c'mon, c'mon!* Takigawa and his people could be closing in on me.

I finally flag down a taxi. I am soaked to the bone and shivering uncontrollably. I twist around to see if we're being followed. I direct the driver to my apartment and tell him to wait. I run into my apartment, grab my passport and my airline ticket, and stuff my suitcase with as many clothes as I can. I duck into the cab and we head for the airport. I know if I stop for a minute, they might catch me. I imagine this guy will stop at nothing to have me taken out. I have seen his illegal operation. He knows I could report him and close him down. I check a couple more times to see if a car is trailing us. I arrive at the airport a little after 10:00 p.m. and sprint to the ticketing area. Winded, I ask for the next flight to LA with any available seat. I brace for the answer. Any delay and the Japanese mafia could kidnap me. I pray as the agent searches. She tells me there is a flight leaving in an hour.

Oh, thank God! "I'll take it!"

The agent takes my open-ended ticket. I hurry through security and board the plane. I take my seat, buckle up, and remember to breathe. I must have been holding my breath the entire time. I can't believe I am safe. I order a scotch on the rocks and then another. I am so relieved. But my relief is interrupted by thoughts of vacating my apartment before he returns to LA looking for me or, worse, sends a hitman.

Watching this scene unfold in front of me, as if it were happening now, leaves me feeling like I shouldn't have taken the risks I did. I am glad I made it out alive. Thanks, Mom, for looking out for me.

Chapter Twelve

Twenty-Six Going on Forty-Five

I call Desiree from LA after fleeing the Japanese mafia.

"Oh, thank God. I've been worried sick about you. Takigawa came into the club looking for you. I told him you had vanished into thin air. So, guess what he did? He cancelled the tour and said I was on my own. Nice, huh? Why did you take off so quickly?"

"What would you do if your boyfriend showed you his sex-trafficking operation? I panicked when I saw the girls enslaved and tripped out on drugs. I didn't want to be murdered because I knew too much or wouldn't help him recruit girls. And who knows? Maybe he would have sold me into slavery."

"Oh, wow. I had no idea he was wrapped up in that. What a nightmare. Listen, I don't want to alarm you, but you'd better watch your back. I've heard he is mafia."

"I know. I will. You too, girl."

I immediately move in with my girlfriend, Veronica. She works as a controller at the company I worked for before I left LA.

My first night back I make us a roasted chicken dinner with all the trimmings. She tells me that Mr. Bernstein wants to talk to me. She thinks he wants to hire me again.

I loved working for Mr. Bernstein, and I was his best leasing consultant. He reminds me of my grandfather. He is an amazing man; not only is he an Auschwitz survivor, he is also one of the largest developers in LA. He owns and operates many multi-family complexes in the greater LA area. I love that man. He is in his 80s, but still gets to work every day by 8:00 a.m.

Veronica calls me at home and tells me to come in at 10:00 a.m. I am so excited to see Mr. Bernstein. I plan to surprise him with a fruit basket from a stand on La Cienega Boulevard. Fruit is his favorite thing.

He seems happy to see me. We talk for hours about his life in Los Angeles and mine in Japan. He finally married Anna, a woman he has been with for more than 20 years. I tell him how different Japan was and how much I missed LA. He says he needs someone to supervise the on-site managers. He doesn't want them bugging him anymore. He tells me the job will include an apartment and a car, because I will be driving all over LA and beyond. I jump out of my seat and give him the biggest hug.

The apartment complexes are scattered throughout the city, from Orange County in the south to Lancaster County in the north. The office is in Beverly Hills, where he lives.

I say, "I promise you I will not let you down."

He responds, "I know you won't."

Then I run to Veronica's office.

She says, "Let's go to lunch. I know a great place on Rodeo Drive — La Scala."

I say, "I'm buying. I owe you big time!"

She smiles.

After lunch, Mr. Bernstein comes into Veronica's office. "Would you please take Jackie to my car dealer to lease a car?"

I say, "Are you sure?"

"You're worth it. I called one of my apartment managers in the neighborhood and told him to lease you some furniture." He hands me the guy's name and address and says, "Call him later today."

I can't believe he is being so good to me. *He must be an angel in disguise sent from God. I just know he is.*

The next day I get to the office early and leave some pastries on Mr. Bernstein's desk. Then I head into the kitchen to brew a pot of coffee.

He comes into the kitchen. "You're here early."

I say, "So are you. Some things never change."

He smiles. "Come to my office. I want to give you something."

I follow him wondering what in the world more he could give me. I just got a beautiful new Saab 900S convertible and an apartment down the street.

He says. "Sit down."

I sit down at his desk with my cup of coffee. He hands me the box of pastries. I smile and take a cheese Danish.

He says, "You're going to need some things for the apartment."

He opens his desk and hands me a company credit card. "Go get what you need for the apartment and settle in over the weekend. I will see you Monday morning at 8:00 a.m. to talk about a game plan."

"Thank you so much. I won't take advantage of it."

He smiles. I leave the office after Veronica arrives. I tell her I will see her Monday.

She says, "Have a great weekend."

"Thanks to you, I will. I won't forget what you've done for me."

I jump into my beautiful convertible Saab and put the top down. I head for Veronica's place to get my things. I feel the sun on my face and the breeze blowing through my hair. I'm so grateful to have the opportunity to work for him again.

Thank you Lord for blessing me. I can't believe after everything I have done that you still care for me. Mom always said I was a child of a King. I feel like a princess. How can I be so blessed? Mom must be pulling strings in Heaven. Thank you, Mom. I miss you so much.

I go to church, for the first time since Mom died. I found a rock-and-roll Christian church in Westwood down the street, or rather, it found me. When I left the grocery store near my new apartment, there was a flyer for the church on my car door. It's nothing like the routine Catholic services I went to as a kid. The contemporary music speaks to my soul. Listening to everyone sing so beautifully around me, it is as if a choir of angels is singing to me. I am overcome by emotion and try to hold back my tears. But the words penetrate my broken heart and tears cascade down my cheeks. I am so grateful I heard the call to come here. A girl taps me on the shoulder from behind and hands me a box of Kleenex. Her smile reminds me of Mom's. In fact, I feel Mom's presence.

I want to know what you believed in so strongly, Mom. I've missed you so much since you left me 13 years ago.

Tears stream down my face. My heart urges me to visit Mom's grave for the first time since her funeral. I am tired of running.

I am sorry I have been so awful, Lord. I've been trying to find my way in a world of darkness — a world without you. I don't want to close my heart off from you anymore. Thank you for giving me a second chance.

I am sobbing. No one approaches me, thank God. It feels good to let the tears come. My heart heals with every fallen tear. I surrender to the Lord and admit that my way isn't working.

I trust you. I don't want to be mad at you anymore. Thank you for not giving up on me.

I am not ready to talk to anyone this morning. I haven't cried this much since mom died. I leave the service before it is over as the congregation sings "Amazing Grace." The lyrics speak directly to my soul.

"Amazing Grace, how sweet the sound, that saved a wretch like me. I once was lost, but now am found. Was blind, but now I see."

I head to my car and drive south on the 405 freeway toward San Diego. Mom was buried in the Holy Cross Cemetery north of San Diego. It's weird. I was 12 years old when I was here last, but I remember the exit as if it were yesterday. The street is Hilltop, which is the same as my old school. I pull into a Chevron gas station to ask for directions to the cemetery. This area has really changed. It was a rough area before, and it has really gone downhill. I feel like I am in the ghetto with graffiti on every abandoned building, lowriders parked everywhere, and Chicanos hanging out in front of the gas station. But I am not afraid. I know God is watching over me.

I pull into the cemetery and park in front of the office. A Spanish-looking man sits behind a desk. "Can I help you?"

"I'm trying to find my mother's grave."

Clearly noticing that I've been crying, he hands me a box of tissues.

"Thank you."

"What's her name and when did she die?"

I tell him her name and that she died in November of 1974.

He looks surprised. I don't blame him, since it has been 13 years. He looks something up and hands me a map of the cemetery. As he circles her gravesite with his pen, he says, "Look for the statue of Saint Michael."

I thank him and walk out. I locate the statue but can't find her grave. I am lost and disoriented walking between the gravesites and reading the headstones of deceased strangers. I am exhausted and am ready to give up. I step over several gravesites to head back to the car when I spot her name. Underneath her name it says, *Loving Mother and Wife.* My knees collapse and I fall to the ground. I am so weak I can't get up. I lie on top of her grave and weep with my head on her gravestone. The warmth of the sun soothes my body.

I miss you so much, Mom. I was so afraid when you died. I couldn't believe that God took you and left us with a madman. I felt so abandoned. I just wanted to die. But I don't anymore. I want to live. I surrender my life to you, God, knowing I can't live without you.

I feel Mom's arms wrap around me. It is as if someone is holding me tight. I cry in her arms until the sun sets. I kiss her name on the gravestone and for a moment I see her face smiling at me.

* * *

My first day of work is great. Mr. Bernstein and I talk about making improvements to the existing apartment complexes. He gives me the contact information for the on-site managers and instructs me to meet with them and walk the properties. I love driving the highways of LA. I know these roads like the back of my hand, having driven them when I was a leasing consultant.

I spend the week meeting with the on-site managers. One says that some of the tenants didn't renew their leases and moved to a newer complex down the street. I walk the complex to identify the required maintenance. The landscaping is in disrepair, so I set up an appointment with a landscape contractor for Monday. Another tells me the other complexes in the neighborhood are newer. I drive to the newer complexes to see what they have that we don't.

The weekend arrives and I'm playing volleyball with the singles group from church on the beach near the pier in Santa Monica. A few guys strum their guitars as people sing along. Everyone brought picnics with tasty sandwiches and other treats. We are basking in the sun eating our lunches. The seagulls are looking for a handout, so I throw them some bread from my sandwich. It's hot, so I slip off my shorts and my t-shirt to reveal my sexy white bikini.

"Who wants to go for a swim?" I shout.

My friends jump up, remove their t-shirts and shorts, and we run into the ocean. As I dive in, I remember that I'm going to be baptized tomorrow. I can't wait! I want to renew my vow to God to reflect his image. He is so worthy of my love. I feel his grace and mercy shining down on me while I am swimming. The waves crash against my body. It's so cold and yet, refreshing. I feel young again. I dive underneath the next wave, and as I am coming to the surface, I feel renewed.

On Sunday the pastor is talking about being baptized after the service. He reads from Matthew 3:11. "I indeed baptize you with water unto repentance. But he that cometh after me is mightier than I, whose shoes I am not worthy to bear, he shall baptize you with the Holy Ghost."

Those words, "I am not worthy to bear," ring true in my heart. I am not worthy to bear all the blessings that God has bestowed on me the past few weeks. I am singing to the Lord from my heart and soul. I feel such peace and love raining down on me. I have a new lease on life.

Michael Landon's wife, Linda, offers her beautiful home in Bel Air for the baptism. Linda is one of many celebrities who go to our church, the "Hiding Place." The church is named after a scripture in Psalms that says, "You are my hiding place; you preserve me from trouble; you surround me with songs of deliverance." I feel delivered. My heart brims with such gratitude. I can't believe that God has blessed me so much. I have a great job and so many new friends who love me as I am.

The swimming pool has large boulders all around it and my friends are sitting and sunning themselves while the pastor calls us into the pool, one by one. He calls my name. I feel like Mom is walking beside me, holding my hand. There is such peace and love in my heart. The sound of the fountain flowing from the rocks into the pool soothes my soul. A friend plays his guitar, and everyone sings along

The pastor asks, "Is Jesus Christ your Lord and Savior?"

I say, "Yes."

He adds, "Then in obedience to our Lord and Savior Jesus Christ, and upon your profession of faith, I baptize you, Jackie, in the name of the Father, the Son, and the Holy Spirit. Amen."

He holds my head back under the fountain while I hold my nose. Then he pulls me back up and out of the fountain, gazing into my eyes, he says, "I have a word for you from the Lord, Jackie," and continues:

"You have been forgiven much, so love much. Go forgive everyone who has sinned against you."

Tears stream down my cheeks and mix with the baptismal water on my face. I know he is talking about my father. *When I get home, I am going to call him.*

My Dad and stepmom live in Washington state now. He got a job at Boeing in Seattle. I dial his number to touch base. It has been so long since we last spoke.

My stepmom answers. "Your dad's not here," Her tone is cold, her pace abrupt.

I'm startled. I want to talk to my dad, but feel the spirit leading me to talk to her instead.

I blurt, "I want you to know that I forgive you for what you did to us when you kicked us out." I can tell she doesn't know what to say, so I continue, "I never told Dad that you gave us our walking papers, and I never will. I know you were probably mad at him for leaving you with us kids. I am sorry. I was so out of control and so mean to you. I was mad at God for taking my mother away and I punished you for it."

She says, "I know you were upset that your mom died, and I didn't know how to comfort you. I am sorry I did that. I was upset. Please forgive me."

"I do. I just wanted to let you know how sorry I am for being so out of control."

"You don't have to say you're sorry, Jackie. Thanks for calling."

I hang up and cry. It feels good to forgive her after carrying around resentment for so long. I had wanted to talk to my dad, but I decide to write him a letter instead.

I make myself a cup of tea the Irish way, by adding a few heaping spoons of sugar and lots of milk. I sit at the kitchen table and sip my sweet, luscious tea. I am reminded of the countless cups of tea my mother made the same way. I feel her with me. The sun sparkles through the window at the sink. The crabapple tree outside my window is exploding with pink blossoms. I love the new beginnings of spring.

I grab a pen and paper and begin writing.

Dear Dad,

How's life treating you on Lopez Island? I heard you retired from Boeing. Hope you are finding lots of time to sail. I think about you often and wish we lived closer. Life is good right now. It hasn't always been. It was hard for me growing up in our home. I do love you, Dad, but you were so angry all the time. I just wanted to get as far away from you as I could. I am done running. I have settled in LA again. I have my old job back. It feels right to be here. I went to Mom's grave the other day. It felt good to be with her. I miss her. I miss you, too.

I would love to visit you soon. I forgive you for being out of control while I was growing up. I know now it wasn't about me. We have a lot more in common than you know. I heard you were molested by a priest that was supposed to take care of you when you were young. That must have broken your heart. It broke my heart to hear it. Mom must have told the older kids and spared us because we were too young. They told me about it a few weeks ago. I am sorry that happened to you. No kid deserves to feel like their parents don't care about them. I felt like that, in a way. Mom tried to make up for your shortcomings, but I just wanted to feel love from you.

I was also molested by Mr. Wilson, the old man down the street, when we moved from Connecticut to Los Angeles. I blamed you for years, but it wasn't your fault. I was in the wrong place at the wrong time. I kept putting myself in harm's way for a long time after that. I didn't feel worthy of love. I went back to church a few weeks ago. I feel like I am healing from my past mistakes.

It feels good to be loved and accepted, with all my shortcomings. I love you for what you are and for what you are not. You will always be my father. I know you didn't know how to love me. You never learned how to love from your parents. That must have been hard being sent to boarding schools and not being allowed to come home for the holidays. No wonder you would get so mad and out of control at the holidays. Call me sometime. I would love to hear from you. Until then, be well and know that you are loved.

Your daughter, Jackie

I can't stop crying. My tears dampen the letter. I wipe them off with a napkin, fold the letter and slip it into an envelope. I lick the envelope and seal the letter. Relief washes over me. It feels good to let Dad off the hook and love him where he is right now. I feel so much love from God, my friends, family, and employer. *Thank you, Lord, for showing me how to forgive my dad.*

> ***It's so weird having this out-of-body experience. I am right here with a younger version of myself. That day changed my life. I learned how to forgive the people who hurt me and let go of the past. I need to forgive myself.***

Chapter Thirteen

Twenty-Eight Going on Fifty

The weight of the world has lifted off my shoulders. For too long, I believed lies I told myself about how I am not worthy of a good life and not lovable or capable of loving. *But I am worthy and capable.* I don't want to go through life with any more regret. I've made some poor choices. It feels good to finally forgive my father and stepmom, but mostly it feels good to forgive myself for what I've put myself through. It's time to start living the life of my dreams.

I met with several contractors about improving the properties and gave the bids to Mr. Weinstein. He says he really appreciates the work I've done the past few weeks and likes having me as his eyes and ears on the properties. He used to go to the complexes himself but hasn't been to them in a long time. He gives me the green light to start on the improvements.

As I'm leaving his office, he says, "I want to talk to you about some new projects after these properties are improved."

I smile. "Sounds good. Go have a great weekend."

* * *

A few weeks have passed, then the start of another. I am involved in several ministries at church and feel so at home with the people here.

For lunch today, I meet a woman named Tracy from church. I really like her and respect how she lives her life. She reminds me of Mom. She's beautiful and has sandy, brown shoulder-length hair with streaks of gray. Her eyes, like mine, are the color of the ocean - sometimes blue, sometimes green, changing with her mood. She leads by example, like mom did.

I share what I've been through and how hard it has been for me. She gazes into my eyes, leans forward, and grasps my hands, as if she is peering into my soul. I see my mom; tears well up in my eyes. At that very moment, an incredible yellow butterfly lands on our hands. Chills course through my body. It's the strangest thing, as it doesn't seem to be going anywhere. It's content just to rest on our hands, fluttering its wings.

Tracy glances at the butterfly. "I want to teach you something."

I listen intently and look deeply into her eyes.

She says, "We are much more alike than you know. The day I learned about spiritual warfare and how to use it was the day I took the reins of my life back. I want to show you how to fight your demons."

I feel the walls crumbling down around my heart. "Please teach me everything you know. I have so many demons to take down."

The butterfly takes flight and lands on a nearby hibiscus bush. Tracy smiles at me. "You're ready for this. I know you are." She continues, "For our struggle is not against flesh and blood, but against the rulers, against the authorities, against the powers of this dark world and against the spiritual forces of evil in the heavenly realms."

"What do you mean?"

"Ephesians 6:12 tells us to put on the full armor of God, so that we can make our stand against the devil's schemes." She adds, "Therefore, take up the full armor of God, so that when the day of evil comes, you will be able to stand your ground."

I close my eyes while she speaks. I see an angel with a huge expanse of golden wings levitating before me. My Mom is here. I can see her so clearly. Tears stream down my face. I gasp for air. It feels good to cry, as if my heart is being cleansed. Tracy puts her arm around me and asks, "Do you have a Bible?

"No, I don't."

She says, "I cherish this Bible. I have had it for 20 years. I want you to have it and read everything I have highlighted. I want you to memorize the scriptures that penetrate your heart. I know the spirit of the living God will be with you."

It occurs to me that she is much older than I am. She must have started doing this at my age. I ask, "How old were you when you started practicing spiritual warfare?"

She says, "I was 28. I am now 48." She can see I am blown away. She looks directly into my eyes and says, "What?"

"My mom was 48 when she died. It was on Thanksgiving Day in 1974."

Tracy is taken aback. She closes her eyes for a second and when she opens them, she is peering down.

"What are you thinking?" I ask.

She looks up. "That's the day I started learning about spiritual warfare. I was at a Thanksgiving Day service at church and the pastor was talking about spiritual warfare. My mom gave me this Bible 20 years ago when I was about your age struggling like you have been."

She takes her Bible out of her purse and shows it to me. I take it and open it up to where she has a bookmark. The papers are tattered and there are highlights over many of the passages. She says, "I didn't start reading it until after that service. I haven't put it down since. I want you to have it."

"Oh, then I can't take this from you."

"My mom told me to give it to you. When you were telling me your story, I felt her spirit as well as someone else's. I think it was your mom. Please take it. It's a gift."

"Are you sure?"

"I am now. It's time for me to pass it on."

I stand up and give her the biggest hug. I say, "Learning to take down my demons is the best gift anyone can give me. I don't take it lightly."

"I know you don't."

I feel like she is an angel sent to me by God.

I go home, make a cup of tea, open the Bible and start reading the book of Genesis: *In the beginning....* I can't put it down. I grab a yellow pad and write down the verses that speak directly to my heart. It's as if this book was written for me.

Any time I catch myself thinking negative thoughts about myself or anyone else, for that matter, I use the scriptures to remind me of God's promises. I also use scriptures when I am praying. I will insert my name in prayer to make it personal. I am a spiritual warrior, taking down the demons that have long haunted me. I will not be stopped. I do not listen to the negative conversations I once had with myself. They were all lies. I have new, wonderful dialogues with myself, like: *I deserve to be happy and loved* and *if I would have known better, I would have done better.* We do the best we can with what we know at the time. Lord knows I've made some awful choices. But one of the best choices I've made lately is hanging out with Tracy. We've become great friends. In fact, she gave me a black-and-white English Springer Spaniel she adopted at the humane society. She originally got the pup for her daughter, who broke out in a rash from head to toe. Her allergy was my good fortune. The spaniel is a fully trained one-year old. The on-site property manager knows how well Mr. Weinstein and I get along, so she said I could keep him. The small yard off my apartment's back patio is perfect for my pup, Patches. It's great taking him with me to the beach on the weekends. He loves to catch tennis balls while running down the beach. The manager has grown attached to him, too. She watches Patches during the day while I am working. I am elated to have another dog. It broke my heart to leave Jacob at home when I was kicked out.

* * *

I am involved in the prison ministry at church. They have several people who write and visit the prisoners at the California Men's Colony in San Luis Obispo, about an hour north of L.A. I was given a name and address of a man name Robert Williams. I wrote him a letter introducing myself and telling him my story. I shared how much going back to church has helped me find some peace. I received a letter from him within a week of my sending mine out. He seems like a good guy who made some bad choices. I get it. I've got my own regrets. He wants me to visit him. I am a little apprehensive as I don't want to get in too deep with him. I've prayed about it. I trust God is leading me to go. It's Saturday, I am following the directions Robert sent me.

It's a cloudy day, but thankfully not raining. I pull into the parking lot and go into the office. There's a sign-in sheet at the desk. There are several people sitting around the waiting room and some outside smoking. I take a seat by an older lady who is waiting to see her son. A few minutes later they call her name and she is escorted out by a guard. I am nervous. I don't know what to expect. I head outside to smoke a cigarette. A gal walks out behind me and asks if she can bum one. I hand her one and light it for her. She looks at me with a sad smile.

I ask her, "Who are you visiting?"

She says, "My old man."

"I'm visiting this guy I met through the prison ministry at church."

She looks at me with a look of disgust, rolls her eyes and says, "Good luck with that," and walks away. *What is that supposed to mean?*

A few minutes later I hear my name over the speaker. I am walking down a long hallway with a guard who doesn't say anything to me other than, "Follow me." He walks me into a room where a woman frisks me. It's strange having someone pat me down, even between my legs and breasts. *I can't believe they can do this.* I don't say anything. I am just standing here with my arms out to my side and my legs open about a foot wide. I'm wearing a skirt. I wished

I would have worn pants. She nods to the guard and he takes me outside where there are round picnic tables with four seats attached. There is a guy sitting alone at the table we are walking toward. He is in good shape. He looks like he works out. There are several tattoos on his bulging arms. He has thinning blonde hair cut short, and a handlebar mustache. The guard instructs me to sit down in the seat across from him and stands about six feet away looking over us.

"You must be Robert." I say with a stutter.

"You must be Jackie," he says, with a smile.

"Don't be nervous. I don't bite." He chuckles.

"This is just so foreign to me. I've never been to a prison before."

"Believe it or not, I'm used to it. It's my home now, whether I like it or not."

"I'm sorry. What did you do to get in here?"

"I was wondering when you were going to ask me that."

"I didn't feel like it was something I should ask in a letter."

"I was high on crack with my buddies and we gang-banged a girl. She was using with us and acting like she wanted it. Later, she claimed it was rape and unfortunately for us, she was 16 years old. I thought for sure she was over 18 and I swear, we didn't rape her."

I'm in shock. I don't know what to say. *Did he have to be so descriptive?*

"I have a long drive home. I'm gonna go."

I get up in a hurry and tell the guard I'm ready to go. I can see Robert is surprised. *I am not befriending a rapist!*

I'm shaken. I light up a cigarette as soon as I walk out the door. It's raining, so I hurry into my car, roll down the window and blow the smoke out. *What are you thinking God? I can't do this!* I start up the car and head home. In the silent drive home, I feel God impressing on my heart to continue to write to Robert. God has forgiven me for so many awful things I've done. I shouldn't be judging Robert, but I can't help it.

On Sunday, the pastor's message is about forgiving those people who have hurt me. A few days later, I receive a letter from him telling me he is sorry for being so honest. He has been leading a group of guys at the prison in a Bible study now for several years and has changed. I want to believe him. He is very convincing. He wants me to visit him again this weekend. I am being asked to go into the lion's den. I must trust God and go.

I wore pants this time. I am not going to be humiliated like I was last Saturday. I see him sitting there waiting in the distance. I'm nervous, but if he was so honest with me, I am going to tell him what happened to me and why I was so upset. We talk for the entire hour. Maybe he is really sorry and has changed. We continue to write and visit for a few months. He wants me to marry him in prison. I feel like I should, as God has blessed me so much. After visiting with Robert again and again, I am driving home on a beautiful Saturday afternoon and my car starts to sputter like I'm breaking down and losing power. I realize the gas gauge is on empty. I pull over to the side of the road. An old guy pulls up behind me in a beat-up pickup truck, walks up to my car and asks me if I'm okay. I tell him I ran out of gas. He says, "It's your lucky day then, as I have a can of gas in my truck." While he is walking to get the gas, I say to myself, *Thank you Lord for sending an angel to help me.* I see him in my rearview putting gas in my car. He walks up to my window and says, "That should get ya to a gas station."

"Thank you so much. What do I owe you?"

"Nothin', I've been wanting to get rid of it. Were ya visiting the prison today?"

"Yes, I was visting my fiancé."

"Well, you're gonna get married? Why, would ya go do something dumb like that?"

"I don't know."

"Well, ya don't have to if ya don't know. You're a pretty lady. Give it some thought."

"Okay, I will. Thanks for everything."

I start up the car and it turns over with a putter. I'm taken aback by what he said to me. *Was God telling me I don't have to marry Robert?* I drive away and see he is still standing on the side of the road waving like my grandparents always did. I stick my hand out the window and wave. I feel like he is messenger from God. I don't have to marry Robert. I was going to for God, but honestly did not want to live a life of visiting my future husband in prison. God is speaking to me. I hear words in my head saying, *You are a child of a King. If you ask me for a fish, would I give my daughter a scorpion? No, I would not.*

I get home and write my last letter to Robert. I tell him I can't see him anymore.

Two weeks have flown by and not a word from him. I think he knows I'm done.

It's Sunday I pull into the parking lot at church and see a cute Asian guy getting off his motorcycle. He's sporting a red bandana on his head, like the one I wore on my head on Thanksgiving, the day Mom died. I am transported back to that day, dressed in my costume and ready to perform for Mom on Thanksgiving Day. I feel her here with me. I smile at him and watch him sit down on the entrance stairs and light up a cigarette. I wish I could do that. I always wait until I am a few blocks from the church. I admire that he can just sit here and smoke his cigarette. As I enter the church and take a seat in the back row, I watch for him. He still hasn't come in by the time the service is ending.

I leave the service a little early and he is still sitting there.

I turn his way and say, "Hey! How's it going?"

"Not bad."

"What are you doing out here?"

"I am listening to the message and the music."

"Why not go in?"

"I don't want the roof to cave in." We both laugh.

"If it hasn't fallen on me, I can assure you, it won't on you."

He smiles.

I say, "A bunch of us are going to the beach for lunch. Do you want to join us?"

He says, "It's a beautiful day for the beach."

I say, "Follow me," and jump into my car. As I am driving down Santa Monica Boulevard toward the Pier Parking lot, I reflect on how he didn't feel worthy to come into the church. I like that about him. I can relate. I never felt worthy, but I went in anyway.

He jumps off his motorcycle. "I'm Johnny. What's your name?"

"Jackie."

He tells me he is from the Philippines. He doesn't seem superficial like so many people in LA. He is not tall, not short, maybe 5' 8". He takes off his black leather coat and reveals a blue jean sleeveless shirt which shows off his muscular biceps. He has jet-black hair, dark-brown eyes, a beautiful smile and a flat, wide nose.

As we walk down the pier, we pass guys fishing and seagulls hanging out waiting for the leftover guts for lunch. The smell of fish and guts mixed with saltwater permeates the air. The sun is shining. I feel like today is the first day of the rest of my life. Anything is possible. We sit down at a picnic table at a restaurant on the pier.

"Where is everyone?" he asks.

"Down on the beach. We can go say hi after lunch."

He lights up a cigarette and asks me if I want one.

"Please."

It feels good to smoke a cig in public. I am such a hypocrite. I usually smoke only at home or in my car when I am alone. I feel like I can be myself around him. I guess that is a good sign. He is a manager at a gas station and lives in East LA. I don't want to be hypocritical anymore. I want to be me.

After our lunch of fish and chips, we head to the beach to meet my friends from church. They invite us to play volleyball. They put us on separate teams, as they need one more player on each side. Johnny's clearly an athlete, as he masterfully hits the ball over the net right toward me. My competitive nature propels me to leap up and strike the ball over the net toward him. When he misses it, I smile and wink.

We go to church together every Sunday. We also go to the singles-group gatherings. Every Saturday single people from church get together to do something fun, whether it's going to a movie or bowling or on beautiful days going to the beach or for a hike. Today, Johnny and I decided to skip it and do something together, instead. It's so much fun riding his motorcycle with him. It feels good to wrap my arms around his waist while we sway left and right as he goes around the curves on Mulholland Drive. Right now, we are headed to the gym. I haven't slept with him and he hasn't pushed it. I like that he is moving slowly. I feel special and safe with him.

He's from the Philippines and moved here with his mom a few years ago. I feel like I can open up to him about my life. I share all the details of my awful past. He doesn't seem to judge me, but when I ask him about his life, he changes the subject. I wish he would share more about his life in the Philippines. But I suppose it doesn't matter. We are here now. I really want to be with him.

With each passing day, I feel more like myself. I'm so happy my identity struggles are behind me. Thankfully, I'm not like the people in this city who pretend to be something they're not. I don't belong here. There is something so phony about LA, except for my church friends and Mr. Bernstein, my boss. Johnny feels the same way.

Johnny and I have been seeing each other for a few months now. We haven't slept together. I want to wait until I am sure about him. He doesn't seem to push the issue about sex either but keeps hinting about marriage. I am a little gun-shy. I tell him I was married before to a guy from Sweden.

He asks, "What happened?"

I say, "I divorced him. He's an alcoholic."

He asks, "Would you marry again?"

I am caught off guard by his question. I don't want to be someone else's green-card wife. I want to trust him, but something holds me back.

I say, "Maybe someday, but not any time soon." I am confused and wonder why he's asking about marriage. I feel the need to get away, so ask God for inspiration about where to go. I pick up the *LA Times* and see an article in the Travel section featuring Taos, New Mexico, in the Sangre De Cristo Mountains, which means Blood of Christ. I feel called to go.

I ask my boss for a week off. He tells me to get the work at the properties scheduled and to ask the on-site managers to oversee it in my absence. I spend the next few weeks scheduling the contractors. I plan to leave the Saturday of Labor Day weekend.

Before I go, Daniel calls and invites me to a barbeque at his place. Dad is coming down from Washington. I can't wait to see him. Meagan is flying in from Texas and Laurie is flying in from Rhode Island. I am excited that we will all be together.

My dad is in town to help Patty move to Washington. She is tired of living in LA and, honestly, I don't blame her.

I love being with Dad and my siblings. We are having the best time we have ever had together. Dad is standing next to Daniel while he grills the burgers. They're smiling and talking more than I have ever seen them. I'm not walking on eggshells around Dad, either. I put my arm around him and tell him, "I've missed you."

"I've missed you, too. Why don't you come up to Lopez Island and visit me soon? I'll take you sailing."

I smile. "I would love that." I breathe a sigh of relief. Maybe now that we are adults living our own lives, it is easier for him to be himself with us. What a wonderful send-off before my road trip to Taos.

Johnny is worried about me driving alone. He has offered to watch Patches for me. I am excited to have the time to think about things without all the distractions in LA. I know God is with me on this sentimental journey. I am reflecting on all that I have been through and where I am right now. I am amazed to see how my life has unfolded in so many miraculous ways. I couldn't have done it without the many angels sent by God. I feel Mom here right now. A tear inches down my cheek.

I drive east on Interstate 10 to 15 north, then east on 40 through Arizona. I decide to take a detour to Sedona, which I've heard is stunning. Checking the map, I see it's just south of Flagstaff, off Highway 89A. I borrowed some camping gear from Johnny, so I could camp rather than stay in hotels. I want to be alone in nature with the Maker and Creator of the universe. I can't believe my eyes when I spot a campground called Banjo Bill's. My grandfather's name is William, but everyone calls him Banjo Bill. I know this is where I am supposed to be, so I stop and find a campsite right on Oak Creek in the Red Rocks/Secret Mountain Wilderness Area. It is late, so I quickly put up my tent and fall asleep to whispers in my heart urging me to leave LA. I know it's the spirit of the Living God speaking to me. And I'm finally listening.

I wake up early to the creek rushing and birds singing. When I peek outside my tent, I see the most breathtaking scenery I've ever laid eyes on. Steep red-rock formations explode out of the earth. I feel small in comparison. I have a heavenly perspective. I can see clearly now, where I am and where I've been. It's as if I am seeing for the first time. I make some coffee over a fire of branches and pine needles. I love the scent of pine branches burning and the crackling sounds when the fire gets hot. It warms me up and takes the morning chill out of my body. I eat the muffin and banana I picked up along the way. After I extinguish the fire and stow my things in my tent, I take a hike. I feel such peace and tranquility as I trek the Bear Mountain Trail. Yellow wildflowers line the trail. They look like sagebrush but have a little yellow flower on the tips of their fernlike branches. It's a beautiful September day and fall is in the air. The trees are gold, bright orange, and red. It reminds me of autumn in New England. The air is brisk yet refreshing. I feel invigorated by the sights and sounds. I can hear the creek in the distance and the birds speak directly to my soul. It's time to turn back and head to Taos. I will come back here someday, I just know it. It's a little glimpse of heaven on Earth. Thank you, Lord, for bringing me here. You are a master painter. What a sacred place you've created here just for me.

I arrive in Taos and head to the Taos Pueblo, the Indian reservation I discovered in the newspaper. I see a sign tacked to the wall offering a spirit ride on horseback. I go inside and sign up for a vision-quest ride in the morning. I can't wait to receive God's message. I come across a beautiful campground near Angel Fire, New Mexico, called Wagon Wheel, and set up camp.

I wake up early and head back to the Taos Pueblo. I can't wait for the spirit ride. The Native American guide tells me to stay silent and listen to the spirit. I choose a black and white paint horse at the barn that reminds me of the horse my dad had as a kid, Tiny Tim; and my black and white Springer Spaniel, Patches. The guide is taking me out to the desert and will leave me for some quiet time. I follow behind his horse, close my eyes and can feel every movement under me of my mount, Rascal. He snorts. I open my eyes and am in the most peaceful place in the universe. The guide turns and heads back to the stables. Birds are singing in the distance and the scent of sagebrush fills the air. The wind whistles through the tree branches. The spirit tells me to get out of the city and find a place where I can be the real me. I would love to live in the country some day and have a horse. I don't know why. I just feel like horses can teach me something about myself. After all, Christ comes back on a white horse. I read recently in Revelation 6: 1-3, in my Bible, *Then I watched as the Lamb opened one of the seven seals, and I heard one of the four living creatures say in a thunderous voice, "Come!" So, I looked and saw a white horse, and its rider had a bow. And he was given a crown, and he rode out to overcome and conquer.*

Knowing now what I didn't then, I would tell that young me, that everything she hopes for is just up ahead. After all Christ rode out to overcome and conquer; so will I.

Chapter Fourteen

Thirty Going on Fifty-Five

After much contemplation during the drive back from Taos, I decided to marry Johnny. He asked me before I left. I told him I would think about it on the trip and let him know. We are getting married on New Year's Eve at my friend, Tracy's house. She just happens to be an ordained minister. I'm dressed in beige jeans, a Western-style blouse and suede cowboy boots. Johnny is in blue jeans, a pressed jean shirt and cowboy boots.

I keep thinking, *why am I doing this?* I haven't slept with him yet. When we kiss, it feels as though I am kissing my brother. I care for him, but there is no passion. Maybe passion will develop with time. I can only hope so. We order Chinese take-out for our few friends who gathered. After midnight, we head back to my place. It is awkward in a way. I don't know who is more uncomfortable — him or me — but this isn't how I imagined it. We are going through the motions of making love, but we are struggling to make it work. We are so exhausted that we fall asleep facing away from each other.

I get up early, as usual. I can't sleep when it's light outside. I brew coffee and whip up some pancakes, scrambled eggs, and bacon. We eat breakfast in bed and talk about getting out of the concrete jungle of LA. We would like to find our Promised Land. Something tells me to call my old girlfriend, Sharon, in South Bend, Indiana. Her dad answers and says she's now living in Colorado with her husband and kids. He gives me her number. I hang up and give her a call.

"Sharon, guess who?"

"Oh, my gosh, girl, it's so good to hear from you! I've thought about you often over the years and wondered where the heck you were."

"I'm in LA and married to a guy from church. What are you up to these days?"

"You'll be relieved to hear I'm staying out of trouble. I got married, too, but in Vegas. We had another baby girl, so now I have two girls. My husband, David, and I started a church in Las Animas, Colorado, and opened a little family restaurant."

"That sounds amazing. I'm so envious! I dream about getting out of LA and living in the country."

"I think I can help make your dream come true. There's a guest house on our property that you and your husband can have."

"What a generous offer! I'd love to be neighbors. I'll talk to Johnny and let you know."

I hang up the phone and tell Johnny what Sharon proposed.

Johnny says, "What are we waiting for? Let's get out of here."

On Monday, we each give notice at work. Johnny sells his motorcycle and our furniture over the next few weeks. I turn in my company car and buy a 1965 Mustang Coupe with a white carriage top and an emerald green paint job. It's got a white pony interior, and a brand-new engine. I couldn't resist! I had some money in a separate account I saved from Japan. We throw bags of clothes into the trunk, put Patches in the car, and head for Colorado. I'm so excited to get out of the city!

We move from LA, the big city of Los Angeles, to LA, the little town of Las Animas, Colorado. It is literally a one-stop town with a gas station, grocery store, a bar, and a liquor store. Most of the commercial buildings are boarded up. I can't believe God's sense of humor. I chuckle to myself.

Sharon's mother-in-law is in the real-estate business in Pueblo, Colorado. She wants me to open an office in Las Animas where Sharon lives, but I need to first take an online course to get licensed in Colorado. Meanwhile, Johnny starts working at the restaurant in Las Animas as a cook. It's exciting to start our new adventure together, even though we are more friends than lovers.

We live on a ten-acre ranch on Highway 50. Sharon and her husband Gerald have all kinds of animals that she got at the livestock auction — pigs, sheep, calves, and a ton of chickens. I want to get a horse but figure I need to settle down first. This city slicker is now a country girl. The church that Sharon and her husband started isn't preaching from the Bible; they teach the Kabbalah, an esoteric school of thought that originated in Judaism. It's too much like the occult for me. Johnny and I don't feel right about it, so we stop going. We don't want anything to take the place of the Christian God we know.

Sharon drinks and disappears for days at a time. She was once a blonde beauty but looks like she's weathered several storms. I know she is up to her old tricks again. It feels like déjà vu. One Saturday, she leaves me with the kids and promises to be right back. She says she is going to the liquor store, but we haven't heard from her in a few days.

* * *

The phone rings while I am feeding her kids. Her husband, very worried by now, answers on the first ring, hoping it's Sharon. She says she's calling from a mental institution in Texas where she is being treated. They talk for a few minutes, then she asks to speak with me. When he hands the phone to me, I go into the kitchen for privacy.

I say, "What's up?"

"I met a trucker at the bar in town who was heading to Texas. He said I could come along for the ride, as he was returning to Las Animas the next day. I just needed to get out of town. But when we arrived in Texas, we got into a big argument; he took off and left me at a truck stop. I had a nervous breakdown right there. I couldn't stop crying and shaking. The attendant called 911 and the paramedics came and took me to the hospital."

"Damn it, girl! You shouldn't have gone with him."

"I know. I had a little too much to drink and wasn't really thinking clearly. They transferred me to a local mental institution, given my history of nervous breakdowns."

"You never told me you've had nervous breakdowns! I'm glad you're okay."

"Gerald is going to come get me. Thanks for holding down the fort, girl. I owe ya."

I hang up the phone. Gerald says he is going to drop the kids off at his mom's place in town and will be back in a few days. *She's crazy. I need some time to think.*

We've only been in Las Animas a few months, but Johnny and I agree it is time to get out of here. I've encountered so much resistance trying to break into the real-estate business. The ranchers don't want to do business with me. They call me a City Slicker, so I've heard. And Johnny gets the cold shoulder in the community because he is Asian.

We take off for Colorado Springs the next day — the nearest big city with more work opportunities. We need to find work quickly. We spent everything but $500 on improving Sharon and David's guesthouse. We trust God will take care of us. Las Animas was nothing but prairies and tumbleweeds, but this feels more like the Promised Land we were looking for. Colorado Springs is booming and beautiful with majestic mountains. It's late October and Pikes Peak is snow-covered. We decide to get a weekly rental at a little motel.

I picked up a free newspaper called the *Thrifty Nickel* at 7-Eleven on our way to the motel and spot an ad for a two-bedroom Victorian house for $400 per month. I immediately call the number when we get in the room and arrange to meet the landlord, a sweet lady named Lois. I tell her we took a leap of faith by coming here, as we only have the first month's rent. I assure her that if she rents to us, we will not let her down. I say we have great references. She takes our application. When she gives us a tour of the house, she's apologetic. The house is in shambles from the last tenant.

"Can we clean this place in exchange for the security deposit, or can we pay you the deposit little by little? Johnny is handy and I know how to paint."

"If you can give me the first month's rent now, you can work off the deposit by cleaning this place up and painting. I'll pay for the paint supplies. I have a good feeling about you guys."

"Thank you so much! You're an angel!"

She is a gift from God, maybe another angel sent to us from God.

* * *

Johnny lands a job as a security guard at a Christian ministry and I found a job in real estate, as a sales trainee. I passed the state exam in Las Animas and got my Colorado real-estate license. Doors of opportunity are opening, and we are walking through them together.

Johnny and I are the best of friends, even though we continue to struggle with intimacy. I've told him everything about me, perhaps too much. Maybe he feels like he could have done better. I just wish he were more romantic.

* * *

After a year in Colorado Springs, we purchase a triplex. My real-estate commission covers the down payment, and the security deposits from the existing tenants cover our closing costs. God is so good to give us the opportunity to own our first place. Colorado is truly our Promised Land. We are blessed.

* * *

A year later we sell the triplex for a heathy profit of $25,000. We find a place in the mountains. It's a little log cabin that sits above a lake in a magical little town called Green Mountain Falls. It's called Lake Gazebo, as there is a white three-rail bridge that leads to a white Victorian-style gazebo in the center of the lake. When the lake freezes in the wintertime, we go ice skating. It reminds me of my childhood. "Isn't life grand?" my mom used to say. Life is certainly grand today. Patches and I are out on the lovely frozen lake surrounded by snow-covered trees and mountains. As I skate, he tries to catch me. I glide across the ice and Patches slips on his paws, but I can see he's having fun. What a wonderful time! Patches fills all the empty spaces in my heart.

* * *

After our first winter of mountain living, we are ready to move back to Colorado Springs. We get more snow here and it's much colder. Also, the commute into town is too much in the wintertime. Today, we got snowed in after going to church in the Springs. The city closed the road to get home, until they clear the road of snow. We are driving to get some lunch in Old Colorado City, when we see an open-house sign. It is a beautiful Craftsman bungalow, a style I love. We decide to go in. The Realtor and his wife just baked chocolate-chip cookies and made a fresh pot of coffee; the sweet chocolate aroma mixed with the rich scent of brewed coffee is divine. We feel right at home and want to stay here forever, so we make an offer. The seller accepts it over the phone with the Realtor. I list the cabin in Green Mountain Falls the next day. I feel so very blessed that we can buy and sell homes, something that was out of reach in LA with the pricey housing market. I am glad we left eight years ago. This truly is our Promised Land.

* * *

Johnny takes off on his motorcycle almost every weekend. When I ask him where he is going, he always replies, "Exploring Colorado!" I stay home and work in the yard. I fell in love with gardening when we first moved to Colorado. I've learned so many valuable lessons while working the soil. I feel connected to God and to the earth. There are so many similarities between gardening and life. I've learned that I must work hard to remove the obstacles that interfere with my garden, like rocks and weeds. Likewise, I have removed countless obstacles in the garden of my life. I must pull all of the weeds, or they will take over. I think of weeds as sin. I am determined to take them out by their roots. I add things to the soil to amend it. Similarly, I amend my heart to make things grow here, too. I am happy in my garden day in and day out. I like to go out at night when it is cooler and weed in the moonlight. It's so peaceful. I am obsessed with pulling the weeds, the sins of my past.

Johnny is becoming more distant to me. I want to have kids, but he has no interest. I haven't been able to get pregnant all these years even though I have never taken birth control. The doctor said it is probably from the infections I had in my youth.

Johnny and I found an inner-city gospel church where we feel at home. The music reminds me of the songs my mother sang to me as a child.

A little mulatto girl named Dina has been coming to church with the pastor and his wife's kids. She lives near them in an apartment complex and plays with the kids in their neighborhood. Her mother and father don't want to take her to church, so she goes with the pastor and his family. Every Sunday she goes up to the front when the pastor has an altar call for prayers. I ask her why she does this, because she is already saved. Dina says she is praying for her parents. She wants them to come to church and give their lives to Jesus.

Dina approaches me this morning. Her hand-me-down clothes hang on her skinny frame. I can tell she wants to say something, but she hesitates. She's sweet, yet insecure. She pulls out a photo from her pocket. It's a picture of her parents, whom I've never met. Her dad is an African American man with a big smile and her mom is a blonde bombshell with a stern expression.

"Your parents look so sweet."

She nods. "Um, would you be my godmother?"

"What a sweet request. But it's not up to me. Your parents must decide."

"If my mom and dad say it's okay, then will you be my godmother?"

"Of course I will." We have become close. I really like her, and she reminds me of myself when I was her age.

The following Sunday, her parents come to church to meet us. Dina nudges her parents to go with her during the altar call. It appears they have given their life to Christ, as they cry when they take their seats in the pews.

Afterward, we go out to lunch together. Dina asks her parents if Johnny and I can be her godparents.

Dina's mother, Nancy, says, "That would be great." Then she turns to us and says, "You two seem like you would make good godparents."

I say, "I can't get pregnant, but I do like kids. Dina is a sweet girl."

* * *

It's late Monday morning, I'm running out the door to the office when I hear the phone ring, so I run back in to answer it. It's Johnny's boss, who asks me to come into his office. When I arrive, his boss says that Johnny has something to tell me. Johnny tells me he's been looking at porn sites on the internet. I'm in shock. *Why would he do that when he doesn't even want to make love to me?* When we try to have romantic evenings, he falls apart and tells me he can't. There's another man in his office who speaks up.

"Hi, I'm Jim Burns. I am the company counselor. Johnny has been frequenting gay porn sites online at his desk."

The counselor claims he can rehabilitate Johnny. I am caught off guard.

"Johnny and I will talk about this later. I have an appointment I am running late for at my office." I run out without saying goodbye.

When Johnny come homes after work, Johnny confesses that when he was a boy in the Philippines, he sold his body to men. No wonder he didn't want to talk about my experiences and would drop the subject when I brought it up; I thought he was ashamed of me, so I quit talking about it. I think our similar pasts would have brought us closer together. If he had told me this years ago when I was spilling my guts to him, I would have felt like we were meant to be together. He has been living a lie.

Feeling so betrayed, I close my heart to him. I thought we loved each other, but, as far as I'm concerned, our marriage is over. I am tired of being used and lied to. He's another one who probably just wanted his Green Card. I can't believe I've been so stupid. *God, how could you let this happen to me? I don't feel I can trust anyone, including You!* I move out of the house in March with nothing but my car, clothes, and Patches.

I am so stressed about my life. Why do I keep choosing the wrong partners? I have lost 15 pounds. I have persistent sharp pains in my stomach that come on quickly like a knife is stabbing me. I used to get sharp pains but only occasionally. My doctor thinks it might be an ulcer, but I think the pain is related to cysts on my ovaries, which I've had for years.

After performing a laparoscopy, a minimally invasive surgical procedure, the doctor says I have endometriosis, a condition in which cells like those in the endometrium, the layer of tissue that normally covers the inside of the uterus, grow outside of it. He recommends surgery. Since Mom died of ovarian cancer, he tells me he may have to do a complete hysterectomy, the surgical removal of the uterus and both ovaries.

I show up at the hospital for my surgery, nervous about the procedure and my future. I feel so alone right now. Johnny doesn't even call me.

Before they put me under, I plead with the doctor, "Please try to save an ovary. I know I haven't been able to get pregnant in the past, but maybe I can in the future."

My doctor says, "My main concern is your life, Jackie. With your mom dying of ovarian cancer, I don't want to save anything if it may cause you problems in the future."

I say, "I trust you."

When I come to after surgery, my doctor is standing by my bedside. He says, "I couldn't save anything."

Through tears I say, "Now I'll never have kids."

"You can always adopt. God will provide a way for you."

I hope he's right.

* * *

Johnny and I are getting a divorce. I am glad I can't have kids. I wouldn't want them with someone struggling with his sexuality. It's October and a month after my surgery. I cry myself to sleep. I trusted that Johnny was the right man for me. We didn't sleep together before we got married, as we put our faith in God. I vow to myself to never marry anyone again without sleeping with him first. *I can't believe God let me marry someone who wasn't even attracted to women. How could I be so blind for the nine years of our marriage?*

Watching this scene flash in front of me, I thought Johnny was the only one that was emotionally unavailable, but I realize now that I was, too. I chose him because he was safe.

Chapter Fifteen

Thirty-Eight Years Young

I've been working for the largest developer in Colorado Springs as a commercial property manager of a Class A office building downtown since the mid-nineties. It's Tuesday, November 7th, 2000, Election Day. I put on my navy-blue suit and vote before I go to work.

A couple hours into my workday, a cute guy strolls into my office.

"Hi! I'm Daryl. My company did the stonework here in the new South Tower construction project."

"Oh, yeah. I know your foreman. He attends the construction meetings with me."

"He told me you need some maintenance manuals for the stone floors and countertops," he says while handing them to me.

I smile and say, "Where have you been all my life? Service after the sale. What a concept." I chuckle.

Daryl is sweet, charming, and a little shy. He is tall and thin and is wearing a light sage-colored suit with a gray tie. He is balding with a gorgeous face and beautiful green eyes. When he gazes at me, it feels like he is peering right into my soul.

"Have you eaten lunch, yet?"

"No, I'm starving."

We walk to the Ritz a few doors away. He is adorable. I don't know why he walks with a limp, but it melts my heart. I don't think he knows how good-looking and sweet he is, which makes him even more attractive. I love his sweet disposition and down-to-earth nature.

"So, are you married?" he asks.

"Not anymore. I was married for eight years. My divorce was final last month in October."

"Oh, I'm sorry."

"Don't be. It's a good thing, actually." And I think, *especially now that I met you*, but I don't say it aloud.

"What about you?"

"I'm going through a divorce now. It's a good thing, too, but not for my kids. It has been over for a long time."

"Oh, you have kids?"

"Yes, two sons — six and almost ten."

"Do you know how lucky you are? I couldn't have kids. We tried, but it wasn't in the cards."

"That must have been rough," he says.

"I've always wanted kids, but now with the divorce, I'm glad I didn't have any. I'm sure kids make it harder."

We talk a little while longer.

He says, "I have to go now, but would love to see you again. Can I call you sometime?"

I smile. It's a big one. "I would like that very much."

* * *

Daryl and I have been seeing each other for a few months. The holidays with him are incredible. We attend his company Christmas party at a high-end hotel. We have so much fun dancing. He wears a gorgeous black suit and a Santa Claus stocking cap. He lavishes his employees with praise and gifts he takes from a tree in the center of the room.

After the party, he books rooms for the employees and their wives who aren't fit to drive home and asks me if I want to spend the night. I drank too much and don't want to drive home, but we haven't slept together, yet. And I'm nervous because I've had lots of abdominal pain since my hysterectomy.

We kiss and cuddle; things heat up quickly. He tries to penetrate me and suddenly I feel like I am going to get sick. I jump up, run to the bathroom, and vomit. I don't know if I am sick from drinking or if there's something wrong because I didn't follow the doctor's orders to rest. I lie on the floor and pray I won't get sick again.

Daryl knocks on the door.

"Are you okay? Can I get you anything?"

"I could use a 7-Up."

He heads to the vending machines down the hall, knocks on the bathroom door and hands me a Sprite. I recover from my sudden onset of nausea and emerge, weary and ragged. We fall asleep in each other's arms. I feel safe and secure in his embrace.

I want to meet his kids, but he would like to wait until his divorce is final. I respect him for his decision, but I dream of the day I can meet them. Then I notice an unsettling pattern. Daryl doesn't take me out in public much, which puts me on edge and makes me doubt our relationship.

In early February, we get in an argument over me being his secret lover. I feel insecure and assume he isn't sure about me.

I say, "Call me when your divorce is final," and he agrees.

I miss him terribly, but it feels like the right thing to do.

On Valentine's Day, I scroll through my emails, and I am pleased to discover an email from Daryl asking how I am.

I write, *I've been thinking about you a lot today. I miss you. How are you?*

He writes, *I miss you, too. Can we try again? Can I take you out to dinner tonight? I want to wine and dine my girl.*

I reply, *I would like that very much.*

We have the most romantic dinner at the Ritz where we had our first lunch.

It's early April and Daryl is taking me camping for my birthday on the 18th. I told him how much I wanted to return to Sedona. He said he found a nice campground close to some great hikes.

We are towing his little travel trailer behind his truck. We've been driving all day and into the night. Even though it's dark, I recognize this road. It's the one I took when I first visited Sedona. When he pulls into Banjo Bill's campground, I can't believe it. I mentioned it to him once before when I said I had to think about my relationship with Johnny. But I never thought he would remember the name of the campground. I'm impressed with his listening skills. He said he found it online and thought it would be perfect because he wants us to think about our future together. He is so romantic.

God, you have brought me back to this sacred place with the most special man. I know I am exactly where I need to be in my life.

We have the most magical time exploring the area and falling deeper in love. It feels like a waking dream. I never thought I could be this happy.

Daryl and I have been dating for about six months and he's finally ready for me to meet his boys. I am nervous, yet excited. I haven't been around kids much and am happy to finally meet them. I want them to like me.

We are at the carnival on a beautiful May day. I love the carnival — the music from the rides fills the air and the scents of cotton candy and popcorn make me feel like a kid again. The sun is shining and it's warm inside my heart. It's so much fun going on the rides together and playing games. I can tell Daryl's oldest son, Kevin, is struggling. He is his mom's crusader, which is to be expected.

His youngest son, Jonathon, is more caught up in the moment. He takes my hand, peers up at me and says, "Will you ride the teacups with me?"

I say, "I would love to!"

We spin the dial in front of us to get the cups to twirl around and around, faster and faster. We are looking right into each other's eyes and laughing so hard. Even though I'm dizzy, I'm loving every minute of it. It's a magical day — what dreams are made of. I can't remember ever being this happy.

Thank You , Lord, for another chance at love. I am sorry I doubted you.

Even though I love Daryl's boys, having them around is a big adjustment. With my life so out of control in my youth, I like everything neat and tidy. I am tired of telling the boys to pick up their things. I sacrifice my feelings for the kids. Daryl defends them when they yell and scream. The divorce has been hard on them.

I realize that things are going to be different with kids around; I must let it go. I need to be more in the moment with them. I wonder if my dad felt like this with us at home. I vow not to be like my father was during my childhood. I am happy my dad and I have a great relationship now. I'm learning to let go of the things that don't serve me. It's time to live in the moment and let go of the past.

I begin to understand and love where the boys are in their lives. I know exactly how it feels to have a strange woman around who's not your mother. I will not be my stepmom. In fact, I promise to be the best stepmom ever. I will never make them feel like they are unwanted.

We have a big beautiful Cinderella wedding on Valentine's Day, a couple of months before my 40th birthday. It took me forever to find the right dress. I decided on an off-white princess gown and a tiara. I feel like a queen. Daryl is dressed in a tux with tails. You know what they say — the third time is the charm.

There was a gaping void in my life until now. I feel so blessed to be a part of raising our kids. Even though I didn't give birth to them, they are my sons. I love their father so much. He has taught me to trust and to open my heart to true love. When all else fails, try, try again. I feel like I am opening my heart for the first time since Mom died, when I slammed it shut.

We are looking for a house near their mom, as we want to be in the same neighborhood as the boys. We find a horse property down the street from where he used to live. I think about how I've been fascinated with horses since

I was a girl when I would ask Mom to stop on the road so we could pet their soft noses. Watching them graze was so peaceful. I relate to them, knowing that horses get tossed from one home to the next. We have a lot in common, closing and then opening our hearts with every new home. I know they have something to teach me. I want one, maybe two or three. I know nothing about horse ownership. I just know I want to learn everything I can from them.

I love animals but have only had dogs in my life. My dogs have brought me such comfort and taught me to love again. Sadly, we had to put my beloved Patches down after he was diagnosed with stomach cancer that spread to his legs. We find a nice pet cemetery in town. The kids, Daryl, and I hold hands around his grave and I say a prayer. We stand there, gazing down, and crying. The boys and I have become much closer. They let me hold their hands on our way back to the car. Patches was the bridge that filled the gap between the kids and me. They loved that dog. When Daryl and I were dating, the kids would ask if I would bring Patches when I came to their place. Patches filled the holes in our hearts, too. I don't want to replace him with another dog. Instead, I would like a horse.

I research horses that are black and white, like Patches. There are Quarter and Paint Horses that are black and white. Then I read about Spotted Saddle Horses, which are docile, kid-friendly, gaited horses. I look online for a Spotted Saddle Horse breeder, and I find one in a small town in Missouri called Saint Mary. I know it is a sign, given that people called my mom Saint Mary. I smile when I think she is still pulling strings for me in heaven. It's as if she wants to gift me my first horse.

The day before Thanksgiving, Daryl and I borrow a girlfriend's horse trailer, hook it up to our truck, and set off to Saint Mary to pick up an eighteen-month-old gelding. The boys are staying with their mother. I feel led to get this gift from my Mom. After a 15-hour drive, we turn on to the dirt road that leads to the farm. I document the scene with my Sony video camera, hanging my head out the window, looking through the viewfinder. It reminds me of the roads in Ohio when Mom and I stopped to pet the horses. In the barnyard in front of a gorgeous old red big barn is a black-and-white pony, like the one my dad had growing up. I jump out of the truck and run over to meet his owner, Christine. She and I have been talking a lot on the phone. She is an angel — sweet with a strong and confident demeanor.

I give her a big hug. She shows us everything she has taught Mack. He was born at midnight, so they named him Stormy's Midnight Mack Attack. His father is a stallion named Stormy. Mack isn't broken to ride, but he has such great ground manners. I can tell he wants to please me. Horse owners usually wait until their horses are two or three years old before they break them. She asks me if I want to ride Stormy to see how it feels to ride a gaited horse. I am a little afraid, as I know stallions can be full of themselves. I only started riding again a few months ago at a boarding facility near our home in Colorado. I rode trail horses when I was younger, but they were old, worn-out types that would follow the butts in front of them. I agree with some apprehension. She saddles him up and I hop on. I can't believe how well-trained he is.

He listens to each of my cues to go faster or slower. I feel I can trust him. What an incredible honor to be on such a majestic creature. His gait is so smooth; there is no bouncing up and down like the Quarter horses I've been riding at the stables. I feel like I am on a magic carpet hovering over the hills behind their barn. Stormy is gracefully gliding back and forth as if we are moving in slow motion yet covering some ground. I return to the barn with a big smile on my face.

"If Mack is anything like his father, I already love him."

She says, "He is exactly like his father. I wanted to keep him until I got your call and heard your story. I knew he was meant for you."

I smile. "I won't let you down. I promise."

In her last letter to me, Christine invited us to spend the night and join her for Thanksgiving dinner tonight. The family are wonderful down-to-earth people. They live and breathe their lives as proud breeders of these incredible horses.

She says, "Mack will teach you a lot."

I say, "Like what?"

She says, "He will be your mirror. He will show you how you are acting and will mimic you, so be confident when you're with him. Move toward your fears, not away from them."

"I will. I promise."

* * *

The next day, we say our good-byes at the crack of dawn. We have a long drive ahead of us.

I say, "I hope I can remember everything you've told me."

Christine says, "Call me anytime with any questions."

We head to the barn, load Mack into the trailer, and set off for Colorado.

* * *

I am learning a lot about horse ownership. It's teaching me so much about myself, too. I went down to the barn to feed him, now named Nizhoni. We changed his name when we put him in our name. Nizhoni is Daryl's Native American name. His mom is a quarter Delaware Indian. His name was given to him by the tribal elders. It means good-looking boy, which is very apropos.

I am up every morning with the birds. I brew some good, strong coffee and head to the barn in my flannel jammies and fluffy slippers. Nizhoni has his butt up to the gate, blocking me from entering. I am afraid to open the gate, as I don't want to get kicked. I remember Christine said I could call her if I have any questions. It's a few hours later in Missouri, so I think I will call her.

I dial her number and she answers, "Hi, Jackie. What's up?"

"How did you know it was me?"

"I have your number in my phone, silly. Is everything okay?"

"Yeah, it's great, but I have a question for you."

"What is it?"

"I came down to feed Nizhoni this morning, and he's standing with his butt toward the gate. He won't let me in."

"He is testing you. You have to take the lead with him, girl."

"What should I do?"

"Hit him on the butt with a stick. He will move away."

"I don't want him to kick me."

"He won't."

I grab a stick from the ground, reach over the fence and smack him on the butt. He jumps away.

"It worked."

"You passed the test. Keep taking the lead, Jackie. You can do this."

"Thank you, Christine. I appreciate it. He's awesome! I do love him."

I hang up the phone and feed Nizhoni.

That evening while I am in his stall cleaning, he puts his butt right up to me and corners me. I lift my hand and give him a little smack on the butt. He runs out, then comes back into the stall a few minutes later. He gives me a nudge with his nose. I think he likes me taking the lead. We are establishing a close relationship. He is teaching me to be more confident and to face my fears. We have learned a lot together. I am going to have him break soon, so I can ride him.

* * *

Spring has sprung in the Rockies. I feel new beginnings are on the horizon for us. Christine and her husband are here to stay for a few days as their kids are out of school for spring break. We are going to break Nizhoni this morning.

I have spent months putting a blanket and saddle on him over the winter. I put my leg in the stir up and gently swing my other leg over the saddle and into the stirrup. I can't believe what a good boy he is. He isn't pitching a fit or trying to buck me off. I guess he trusts me. I'm directing him with nothing but his lead line that

Christine fastened to both sides of his halter. He is so good to allow me to ride him around the barnyard. It is a privilege to be on his back. I love him!

Christine says, "It's time for you to learn to put a bit in his mouth."

She shows me how to hold the headstall with one hand and with the other hand on the bit, she slides the bit into his mouth. She makes it look so easy to do, so I try it. I put his bit in his mouth, his head stall over his head, and fasten the buckle. I mount him and ride around the backyard.

"I think he likes to be ridden. I may take him on the trails nearby."

"You should. There's no time like the present! I'm proud of you two."

I'm afraid to be out of the fenced area. I remember Christine told me to face my fears. The sun is shining, and a gentle breeze is blowing. I've done everything she's told me to do. I trust she knows what's best. I head for the trials nearby at a faster pace than we did in the yard.

Christine smiles. "Have fun!"

I'm nervous, but I don't want him to know, so I take a big deep breath and release it. "If I'm not back in an hour, come looking for me."

She chuckles. "You'll be fine."

We walk down the street where I've been taking him to graze in a vacant field by our house. He bows his head toward the grass, but I lift it with the reins, so he knows not to eat while I am riding. We turn off the road at the end of the cul-de-sac and onto the trail that leads to Palmer Park, with some 32 miles of trails. I know all the trails like the back of my hand, as I often hike here.

I decide to stay on an easy trail near home, so if anything happens, someone may see me. Nizhoni lets out a snort. He tries to pick up the pace, but I tighten the reins. He immediately slows down. It is amazing to be on his back, feeling his legs moving under me. I like the thud, thud, thud of his hooves hitting the dirt trail. I am breathing a little easier, as he hasn't given me any reason to be nervous. It's scary riding alone, but I have learned to move toward my fears, unless there is a reason to move away. Nizhoni has never given me any reason not to trust him. I can't believe I am riding these trails alone, but it's so freeing. I sigh with relief.

I don't want to push my luck, so I turn around to head toward home. Nizhoni speeds up, so I pull back on the reins and say, "Whoa boy." He stops and lets out a snort as though he is saying, *Let's get the show on the road.* I chuckle, release the reins, and give him a little squeeze to go. He walks this time at a slower pace. I lean over and stroke his neck. "Good boy." It feels good to trust again. I think this may be the first time I really have trusted anyone since Mom died. *Thanks, Lord. There is hope for me yet.*

The next day, as Christine is about to leave, I tell her we would like another one of her incredible equine creatures.

She says, "I have a pretty little filly named Angel who I will break this summer."

I say, "Send me a picture of her. If she is anything like my boy, I want her!"

"She is from the same parents as Nizhoni, but she doesn't have spots."

"If she comes from the same parents, I want her."

She smiles. "I'll get her ready for you. You can come get her at the end of the summer."

I can't wait. It will be so much fun to have another horse, so Daryl and I can ride together. He is a Colorado cowboy after all and a natural horseman. Plus, he loves Nizhoni.

Seeing me riding Nizhoni for the first time, I remember the accident now. I am suddenly aware that I am in a state of unconsciousness. I want to wake up and go home to my knight in shining armor.

Chapter Sixteen

Forty Going on Thirty-Five

The summer flies by. It's early September and we are heading to Missouri to get Angel. As we set out, the sun tries to peek out of the clouds. Later, the clouds fade away and it warms up. The road is empty, so driving is relaxing, almost meditative. We leave our hotel early so we can get to Christine's as quickly as possible. We are so excited for Nizhoni to have company in the barn, and not just any company, but his full sister. I'm sure they will adore each other.

Daryl says, "It will be great to have something we can do together."

I say, "I can't wait!"

We arrive earlier than expected. Christine is in front of their gorgeous, big red barn, hosing down Angel. She looks over and waves. We park our truck and trailer.

As we approach her, you can see her big, heartfelt smile. "I wanted to have her all prettied up before you got here."

I say, "We couldn't wait to get here, so we put the pedal to the metal."

She laughs. "Well, this is as good a time as any for you to get to know your girl. Grab a sponge out of that bucket over there and get the dirt off her back."

I smile. "My pleasure."

She is much smaller than Nizhoni when we got him. She's pretty with a shiny brown coat and a perfect white star on her forehead. She is so sweet.

I say, "I'm excited to ride her."

Christine says, "Let's put her back in her stall and let her dry while we have something to eat. We can take a short ride after dinner."

I say, "I can't wait!"

We walk up the dirt driveway by the barn that leads to the house.

Christine says, "I made some fried chicken and potato salad. I hope you're hungry."

Daryl says, "We are. I wanted to stop for lunch, but Jackie couldn't wait to get here. We had a big breakfast at the hotel, though."

We sit down at her kitchen table and enjoy the most delicious meal.

I say, "I love your cooking, girl."

She smiles. "It's my mom's fried chicken recipe."

There's a pitcher of lemonade on the table, so I pour some into my Mason-jar glass. I love everything country. I ask Christine where Rick and the kids are.

She says, "They're at soccer practice. I packed them a picnic basket."

I smile. "You spoil them rotten."

She chuckles. "They're worth it."

After dinner we head down to the barn and Christine asks me to saddle up Angel. She disappears into the barn and returns carrying her saddle. Then she goes back into the barn and brings out two more horses for her and Daryl to ride. Daryl's is a big horse named Renegade.

Daryl says, "The only horse I like to ride is Nizhoni. Is Renegade a good horse?"

She says, "He's Nizhoni's granddad. He's a good ol' boy; you'll love him."

Christine and I saddle up the horses and get on ours. Renegade is such a tall horse Daryl jumps high to mount him. He falls off the saddle on the other side and lands on the ground next to him. Renegade doesn't move, and we all laugh, including Daryl. It looks like Renegade is laughing inside and probably thinking, *these city slickers are funny.*

Daryl dusts himself off and tries again. This time he lands squarely on the saddle. He's clearly proud of himself. "He looks like a good horse, since he didn't budge when I fell at his feet."

We chuckle and head out to the woods behind the barn. I love the scent of moss and pine needles permeating the air. The ground is wet from rain the night before, so we ride at a walk, the horses' footsteps sloshing on the muddy trail.

"These horses are great on their feet," I say.

Christine says, "They are as good as mountain goats, very surefooted. They'll go anywhere you want."

"Sounds good to me," I say.

I've been talking to Christine by phone a lot over the past few months. She has been sharing the progress she's made with Angel and that she's a good ride. I trust Chris. She has taught me a lot about horse ownership since we got Nizhoni. She is a great horsewoman and just a good person all around.

Owning horses is a lot of work, but it's worth it. They teach people a lot about themselves. I think of Nizhoni as a sort of messenger from God who shows me how to be. Horses want you to be present and fair, but firm. I've come a long way since we started "horsing around" a few years ago, and I am looking forward to learning more.

Angel is courageous for such a young horse; she wants to lead the pack. I pull back on the reins to get her to slow down and follow Christine. She obeys my cue and slows down.

I say, "I really like her. She is a sweet little horse."

Christine says, "You will love her. She is a real good horse."

I am excited to have two of Christine's horses. Her dad started breeding horses when she was a baby. She learned to ride at six years old. I wish I had started earlier.

The next day we head back to Colorado with our new little mare in tow. Angel loads right up into the trailer as if she has done it a million times before. I am amazed by how well-behaved Christine's horses are. She is an excellent trainer. I give her the biggest hug and jump in the truck. She stands and waves as we drive away with a big smile on her face.

We stop half-way at a ranch in Salina, Kansas, to spend the night and let Angel out of the trailer. She has been in there for nearly eight hours. Christine told us about this ranch when we came to get Nizhoni. It's a home with a guest house and horse stalls. It's perfect for us. Angel emerges from the trailer and looks around with an expression that says, *this isn't my home.* She looks a little weary. I am glad we're stopping so she can rest for the night. We take her into the stall the ranch hand shows us.

We decide to get some dinner before we settle in for the night. There is an old schoolhouse converted to a barbeque buffet restaurant. It's a one-room schoolhouse, like the ones featured in old western movies. The smoke billows from the smoker out back. You can smell it for miles. It smells delicious. We can't wait to get inside and sink our teeth into the ribs. Christine said they were the best and she was right. I have never had ribs that just fall off the bone like this, and the barbeque sauce is divine. It's all-you-can-eat, including barbequed ribs, brisket, and side salads. We help ourselves to a second serving. The broccoli salad is delicious. It's made with cashews, giving it a salty, crunchy texture with a sweet, tangy sauce. I sure like country cooking.

When we get back to the ranch, I check on Angel and give her some more hay and a scoop of oats. She didn't eat much while we were on the road. I look down into her stall at the nearly empty water bucket. She must have been thirsty. I fill it to the brim with fresh water from a nearby hose, give her a kiss, and tell her I'll see her in the morning.

My sweet hubby Daryl did most of the driving yesterday. He snores the minute his head hits the pillow. It sounds like sawing logs. It doesn't bother me at all, though. Before I know it, I fall fast asleep. We sleep like babies. I didn't realize how tired I was.

The next morning, the ranch owner's wife serves a big country breakfast on the front porch with warm blueberry muffins, fruit salad, and scrambled eggs with chunks of ham and melted cheese, and a thermos of piping hot coffee. It hits the spot — breakfast of champions. We're ready for the last leg of our journey west toward beautiful Colorado.

Thank You, Lord. Be with us on our journey home.

I remember this moment, as if it were yesterday. I miss Daryl, the boys and our equine kids so much. As much as I will miss my mother, I want to live the life of my dreams and go home.

Chapter Seventeen

Fifty-two Years Old

We ride as often as we can before winter sets in. It has been a long autumn. Normally we get our first snowfall by the end of October, but it is already early November and still so beautiful. I love Indian summers. The trees and shrubs are brilliantly colored with the change of season. The scrub oaks have turned a gorgeous bright red. The towering aspen trees in our backyard take my breath away, their amber leaves shimmering in the sunrise like gold nuggets. They leave a trail of amber glitter on the ground. When the wind blows through the leaves, it is as if I can hear maracas playing. I dread the approaching winter. But today promises to be a lovely day. Perfect 65-degree temperatures are in the forecast. A great day for a ride!

We head down to the barn early to feed the horses before we ride. The four-stall barn is white with hunter-green trim pieces shaped into large X's painted the same color as the trim. The color scheme matches the house. Our home has burgundy brick on the bottom with white siding on the top and green shutters with window boxes filled with fuchsia geraniums. The property is in the center of town and sits on more than an acre of land.

It backs up to Palmer Park with more than 800 acres of equestrian trails overlooking Pikes Peak and the Garden of the Gods. Our home is a '70s-ranch style with a full walk-out basement. You can see unobstructed views of Pikes Peak out of every window facing west. We call it "The Ranch."

We grab a cup of coffee, take off our slippers, and slide into our clogs by the back door before heading out to feed the horses. We are still in our flannel jammies. It's real private in the back of the house. The property is lined with scrub-oak shrubs on each side; a grove of aspen trees stands in the middle of the back yard. We have a large arena to exercise the horses and a nice-sized corral outside the barn. We love having the horses in our back yard and feel so blessed to live here.

The horses hear us and neigh, letting us know they are glad to see us. We head to the hay barn — twice as tall as the horse barn — and break open a new bale. I feed my girl, Angel, and Daryl feeds his boy, Nizhoni. I glance at Daryl and his boy, a black and white gelding, admiring the gorgeous view. I think back to when we first met and, although I was immediately attracted to him, I didn't like his clinging-onto-his-thinning-hair look. I could tell with his olive skin from his Italian and Navajo heritage, chiseled face, high cheek bones and full lips that he would be just as handsome with a shaved head or closely cut hair. A few weeks after we started dating, I suggested that he shave his head or cut his hair close to his head to show off his gorgeous face and piercing hazel-green eyes. He shaved his head the next day. It made him so sexy and so much more attractive, which I didn't think possible. He's my Italian Stallion.

While the horses munch on their hay, I cook up some bacon and eggs. It is a bit nippy outside, so Daryl hops in the shower to warm up. I'll shower after our ride.

Last year, Daryl sold his construction company of 30 years and retired at 48. At the same time, I stopped selling real estate so I could slow down and enjoy life with him. We are having so much fun together. *Thank You, Lord, for blessing us.*

The boys are doing great, too. Kevin graduated from college last year with a degree in business management. He is a project manager at a large construction company in Denver. Jonathon is in his last year of college. He is studying business, as well. The apples don't fall far from the tree. They live in Denver together with their buddies from high school. I am so proud of them. It wasn't always this easy, but over the years we have really grown close. Although I am not their maternal mother, I am their other mother. You can never have too many moms. I gave up hope of having kids after my total hysterectomy, but now I have two beautiful stepsons. I love them as if they were my own.

Thank You, Lord, for making something beautiful out of something I felt was so hopeless.

We head down to the barn and saddle up the horses for a short ride in the park. I feel so blessed; I could just burst with joy. Daryl jumps on Nizhoni and heads for the trail. I follow on Angel. The horses are spirited and full of themselves this morning. We should have lunged them in the arena before riding to make sure they were giving us the lead.

The air is brisk; winter is nipping at our heels. More leaves litter the ground than the last time we rode, the crunching underfoot is constant. I am saddened to see the almost bare trees, signaling the end of fall. Oh well, I am happy we are taking the time to ride. With winter around the corner, we won't be riding much. The wind whips in gusts; it feels like it might rain. I should have worn a coat. I shiver, trying to shake off the cold.

Daryl picks up speed on Nizhoni, who breaks into a canter. He knows better than to run toward the barn. But Nizhoni won't resist. Like Daryl, he was born with the need for speed. Daryl bought himself a classic Ferrari when he retired and loves to zip around town in it. Boys will be boys! I move into a canter trying to catch up to them and then break into a full-blown gallop. This is what dreams are made of! I feel like I am riding a magic carpet soaring over the earth. I hear a dog barking in the distance. It gets louder the faster we run. I soon discover a dog is running full speed toward me. I turn to face it, so Angel doesn't get spooked, but the dog doesn't back down. It's a scary looking Pit bull mix. I ride toward the dog to scare it away, but that doesn't work, it only provokes it more. The dog jumps up on Angel's chest, trying to bite her. Angel paws the dog, by picking up her front legs to push the ferocious dog away. I have never seen a dog acting so aggressively. I'm panicking. I don't know what to do.

Daryl must have realized I was not behind him; he is riding back toward us, thank God. Maybe he can scare the dog away. He tries to run over the dog, but it just runs out of the way. The dog darts around to Angel's back side, still trying to get a piece of her. Angel kicks her back legs out but misses the dog. She moves to a full-blown buck and won't stop when I pull back on the reins. I am trying to hang on. My heart is pounding right out of my aching chest. Without thinking, I let go of the reins to grab my throbbing arm. Angel bucks again and I hurl through the air, hit the ground with a thud, and bounce up like a ragdoll.

* * *

Somehow, I can see everything perfectly from a bird's-eye view. It's as if I am watching a television program, but I am in the TV and can't get out. Angel takes off at full speed toward home. The dog chases her. Daryl jumps off Nizhoni and ties him to a tree. A woman sees us in the distance and runs toward us. Daryl realizes I am unresponsive and feels for a pulse. Not feeling one, he immediately starts chest compressions. We took CPR last year. He puts his fingers together, exactly as we were taught. His fingers are intertwined like when we were kids and played, *here is the church, here is the steeple.* He holds his hands and presses continually with his palms on my chest. He continues the chest compressions, desperately trying to get me to respond, but nothing. The lady says she is a nurse and asks him to call 911 while she continues to perform CPR.

His hands are trembling as he talks to God. I can even hear what he is thinking in this ethereal place.

Please, God, be with my wife.

When he dials 911, he explains everything in a panic.

When he hangs up, he takes over the chest compressions to give the nurse a break, his hands still shaking. A siren whines in the distance and is quickly approaching. It speeds into the park and onto the trail toward us.

Please, God, help my wife. She is the most important person in my life, and we can't lose her, Lord, Daryl prays to God.

The EMTs jump out of the ambulance, hauling a gurney. They gingerly lift me onto the gurney and wheel me into the vehicle.

The nurse takes one of the EMTs aside and says, "I was walking when I saw this lady thrown off her horse who was being attacked by a dog. She was unconscious and not breathing, so I performed CPR."

He says, "Thanks a lot for doing that. You may have saved her life. She is breathing now."

Daryl asks, "Where are you taking my wife?"

He shouts, "We are going to Penrose Hospital Emergency."

Daryl says, "I'll be there after I take my horse back to the barn."

Daryl thanks the nurse for helping him, jumps on Nizhoni, and gallops toward the barn. As he rides away, he thanks God for sending an angel to help him administer CPR. Thankfully, we were on our way home, so he gets home quickly. There's no sign of Angel, but he sees the dog limping away in the distance. She must have nailed him, finally. He prays that she is okay and thinks, *Jackie will be devastated if anything happens to her.* He then spots Angel grazing in the field by the barn. He runs to her, grabs her broken reins, takes off the tack, and throws it onto the ground outside the stall. Then he jumps into his truck and heads to the hospital.

Please, God, be with my wife. May she be all right.

He rushes into the emergency room. Winded, he says to the receptionist, "An ambulance just brought my wife here."

She hands him some forms and asks him to fill them out.

"Can I please see my wife first? I just want to know if she is okay."

She says, "She is with the doctor. He'll be out to talk to you as soon as possible. I need your information, so we can help you."

He sits down to fill out the forms, but his hands are shaking. *This isn't happening. It's a bad dream. Calm down. You can do this. Please, God, don't let anything bad happen to my wife and our beautiful life. You can do this. Focus on filling out the forms.*

After completing the forms, he hands them to the receptionist. She looks them over and asks him for his insurance card and ID. He fumbles through the cards in his wallet and hands them to her. He hopes she doesn't notice that he's trembling.

He says, "Can you please find out what is taking so long?"

As she's scanning the cards, she says, "I know you're concerned, sir. I'm sure someone will be out soon."

He sits down quickly, feeling lightheaded, like he might faint. What seems like an eternity is less than an hour.

A doctor with a tanned, weathered face approaches him and extends his hand. "I'm Dr. Parker. Are you Jackie's husband?"

"Yes. Is she okay?"

"Your wife had a heart attack and went into cardiac arrest. She's unconscious, but stable."

Daryl says, "Oh, I had no idea she had a heart attack. Can I see her?"

"Yes, but she won't be responsive because she's in a coma."

Daryl presses. "When will she come out of it?"

"It's hard to say. Sometimes people come out right away and sometimes they don't." He pauses, then continues, "Come with me."

Together they enter my room. Daryl says, "It looks like she's sleeping. Can she hear me?"

"No, but you can talk to her if you want," he says with a smile and then slips out.

Daryl says, "I want to hold you and never let you go. Do you hear me? I love you so much. Please come back to me, Jackie. Please wake up." His face is drawn and he's on the verge of crying. He tries to keep from thinking the worst but fears he may lose me.

He rests his elbows on his knees, his hands on his head, leans over, and prays. *Please, God, be with Jackie and bring her back to me.* He remembers my wishes about being on life support — I don't want to be on life support. *I could never take her off. I will not leave here until she walks out the hospital doors with me.* He weeps, gasping for air.

As if Daryl's tears are cleansing me and bringing me back to life, I feel myself returning to my body. Moments before, I was having a heart-to-heart talk with my mother in a beautiful garden in a heavenly place. When I open my eyes, a bright white light hanging over my hospital bed almost blinds me.

My husband quickly wipes away his tears. "Jackie?"

"Yes, my love?" It hurts my throat to talk.

"Oh, thank God, you're back! I can't believe you've come back to me!" He kisses me on my forehead and cheeks and looks right into my eyes.

"What do you mean? Where was I?"

"You were in a coma."

"I was?"

"Don't you remember the accident?"

"I don't remember anything, except for a dog chasing Angel."

"You fell off Angel."

"Is she okay?"

"She's fine. I'm just so thankful you're all right!"

"Me, too."

A nurse enters my room, sees that I am awake, and scurries out. A few minutes later the doctor comes in.

"How are you feeling, Jackie?"

"I feel a little foggy and real achy. How long have I been here?"

"You've been here for several hours. We thought it might take longer for you to come around, but I am so relieved that you're okay. You must have had a heart attack and fell off your horse."

I say, "What? I had a heart attack?!"

"Yes, and it's a miracle you're awake. Sometimes people don't wake up from comas for a long time. Sometimes they never do."

"Well, my whole life has been a series of miracles," I say, smiling at the doctor.

He returns my smile. "You must have an angel watching over you." He winks and leaves.

The nurse, now standing at my bedside, says, "We are all so relieved to see you awake. We are going to need to run some tests, but for now, can I get you anything?"

"I could use some water. My mouth is dry. It's hard to talk with these tubes in my nose."

"They need to stay in for now, but you can have some water." She leaves and returns with a plastic container of water with a straw coming out the top of it. She hands it to me.

I look into her eyes. "Thanks for everything. I truly appreciate it."

She smiles and says with a Southern drawl, "Yawl are very welcome, my dear," and leaves again.

In the silence that follows, I turn inward. I've always wondered if there was someone watching over me. I felt so alone for the longest time, but somewhere deep inside, I knew I wasn't. I was always being watched or even led by an unknown presence. I now know the powerful presence I tried to disregard for so long was my mother. Even though I suspected it, I would shake off the feeling because it hurt too much to think about her. Eventually, it led me to change my life and start making better choices. I heard the still, small voice inside, saying things like: *You are better than this,* or *Don't act like that.* Even when I didn't think I was being cared for; I was. I know beyond a shadow of a doubt that my ever-present Mother, all-loving Angel was guiding and protecting me.

Thank You, Lord.

Daryl holds my hand. I can feel our hearts embrace.

I say, "I have a new lease on life. Thanks to my archangel, my mother, all my prayers have been answered, all my dreams have come true. I truly can't ask for anything more."

My beautiful husband squeezes my hand. "Me too!"

A few minutes later the boys arrive with the most beautiful bouquet of flowers. Jonathon sets them on the tray in front of me and leans down to give me a hug.

Kevin says, "How are you? My dad said you were in a coma."

"I guess I was, but wild horses couldn't keep me away from you guys."

He smiles. "Don't pull a stunt like that again."

Among the flowers in the bouquet I notice a yellow butterfly made from feathers. "Wow, these are gorgeous. Thank you, guys."

I don't dismiss the butterfly, knowing it's not a coincidence. I remember what my mother said to me about butterflies. *I feel you here, Mom.* A tear trickles down my cheek and into my mouth, the salty taste harkening back to our time at the shore.

"Honey, I'm feeling sleepy. Take the kids to the cafeteria to get something to eat. I'm going to take a little nap."

Daryl bends down and kisses me. As I close my eyes, I hear my mom softly whispering in my ear:

> *I knew I could take a leap of faith into the void and that God would be there to catch me. I did not fall. I am in the heavens with a greater perspective — a heavenly view. I can see Both Sides Now, the end from the beginning, and the beginning to the end. I am here with you now, Jackie and will be with you*

until we are joined for eternity. The spiritual world is more real than anything you will experience on Earth.

Life is but a moment, but the heavenly world is eternal.

EPILOGUE

The winter has come to an end. It was such a time of going within and reflecting on my life over the past six months since my accident. Spring has sprung in the Rockies with such promise of new beginnings. I didn't ride over the winter like I normally do. It was a particularly cold and snowy winter, which gave me plenty of time to nest. I was ready to get back in the saddle to get the horses out of the barn. In the past month or so I noticed Angel was thinner but attributed that to Nizhoni woofing down his hay while Angel took small bites from their shared hay feeder. She would stand there chewing her bites slowly, savoring its flavor. Our first ride was early in May. Angel was sluggish, unlike her brother who was roaring and ready to go. She was struggling to keep up with his fast walk. She was getting winded and breathing heavy, so we made it a short ride. I thought perhaps she was just out of condition like her mother. I was feeling sluggish, too. I haven't wanted to ride but Daryl knew I had to get back on her evidentially. I was glad I did, but even happier that we made it a short ride. I called the vet to schedule spring shots and told her about how Angel was doing. She said she would draw her blood to see what's going on with her. A few days after the vet drew her blood, she called me saying that Angel had a bad liver infection and she was anemic. She wanted me to start her on a round of antibiotics for the next 21 days. I rushed over and picked up the medication and stopped by the feed store on my way home. I bought all kinds of treats and sweet feed as well as vitamins and supplements to help boost her immune system. For the next three weeks, I just loved on her with every goody I could find like apples and carrots. She was in her glory getting all my attention. The vet came out and drew more blood after she finished her round of antibiotics. She called me the next day and told me the infection had gotten worse and her red cell count was dangerously low. She wasn't able to fight off the infection with being so anemic. My vet wanted us to take Angel to a specialist in Denver that could do an ultrasound and run more bloodwork. I was panicking as she insisted, we take her that day and that she would call ahead and let them know we were coming. Darryl rallied as he was equally concerned about her. We loaded her up in the trailer and headed to Littleton Equine Hospital. When we arrived, we thought we were at Graceland as it looked very much like an Antebellum Plantation with its sprawling buildings that read Palliative Care and Intensive Care Unit. I had a knot in my stomach. A vet assistant came out and took Angel back into the facility. We weren't allowed in with the Covid-19 pandemic, they were limited access to the employees only. She was sweet and assured me that Angel would be in good hands. We waited patiently in the truck until Tinker wanted to get out of the vehicle. We were parked by a grassy area, so I let her out. A few minutes later I could see the vet coming out with her assistant leading Angel. Daryl and I stood patiently waiting to hear what she had to say. She said, you have such a good horse. We usually have to sedate horses to run this test, but she just stood there willingly. We both smiled, I said "You do not get a better horse." The vet went on to say that she had terminal cancer. There were several masses on her spleen and one on her heart. It was inoperable as these organs are so vascular. She was afraid if she tried to remove the tumors, she could bleed out and die during the surgery. She refused to do it. We were both in shock that there wasn't anything we could do. The vet prescribed Prednisone to slow down the process of the tumors growing. The side effects were awful though as she could get inflammation in her legs and feet which is painful. It would hinder her mobility. I didn't want to do that to her, as she needs to be able to walk to eat and drink. The poor thing. I just wanted to take her home and love on her, which is exactly what we did. She wasn't refusing to eat anything, but she was getting thinner. I started her on Equine CBD which she responded to very well. She was her frisky and playful self. I wanted a second opinion, as I just knew she was getting better. We made an appointment with another Equine Hospital east of us, in Peyton. The doctor drew her blood to compare to the other two I had from our veterinarian. He also did an ultrasound. He called us in to look at the images. I just knew it was going to be the miracle I was looking for. The vet was very concerned and sympathetic as he said her tumors were getting bigger and red cell count was much lower. He was surprised she could even stand in the trailer ride out here. We were both in shock, as he recommended, we put her down right away. Daryl wanted to bring her home and come back with her brother the next day, so he could be with her when she left this world. We tried to load her many times, but she refused to get in the trailer, which was a first. She always just loads right in. I knew it was her way of telling me she was ready to go home to heaven. Daryl was really struggling with it, but I knew we had to let her go. We walked her out to a beautiful pasture. The sun was shining, it was a gorgeous day. She put her head down and nibbled at the grass while I recited a poem I wrote several years ago.

When I go home to heaven, I know what I will find. God says I'll find a mansion, but a country home will do, just fine. The yard is filled with flowers for all the birds and bees. The porch is warm and roomy, you know that's where I'll be. The kettles always whistling. Come sit with me, upon my porch and help me sip some tea.

The vet gave her the first injection to make her sleepy. She laid down in the tall grass by me. I laid beside her and looked into her dark brown eyes while he gave her the second injection, which would take her away from here in body. Her eyes connected with mine and at that moment I saw her in there, and the next, she was gone. Now I know why they say the eyes are the window to the soul. I saw a flash of light. She released her Spirit into the arms of God. I just laid there with my head in the crook of her neck. Tinker came up and laid down on top of Angel. Daryl stood over us crying and gasping for air. I got up and gave him a big hug and we cried in each other's arms for a while. It was very heartfelt. We drove home in silence. When we got there Nizhoni was running the fence and whinnying when he heard the trailer rattling as we approach the house. He was continuing to whinny and run the fence when he saw he was alone and there was no Angel. At that moment, my cell phone rang. I saw it was the guy I gave a horse to as a companion to his other horse who was alone on 80 acres with two ponds a few years ago. He explained that his horse had died a few months ago and that the horse we gave him, Amber was very lonely. She just stood out in his pasture with her head hung down. He was going to give her away but wanted to call to let us know. I made that a condition upon giving her to him, as I always loved her. She couldn't keep up with our gaited horses Nizhoni and Angel on the trail and she was allergic to something in our barn. She was losing a lot of hair when we had her. She thrived out at pasture. I would visit her often over the years on my way to the feed store. It's funny, he called as we were going to go visit Amber after with Angel. The vet in Peyton is around the corner from her. We decided against it after we put Angel down, as we wanted to get home to Nizhoni right away. It was a miracle he was calling. I handed the phone to Daryl. He couldn't believe the guy was calling us at the exact time we needed to calm Nizhoni. We drove out there right away and loaded her up in our trailer and brought her home. It made the day so much more bearable just knowing they had each other to comfort. She was so happy to be home and Nizhoni was beside himself when she popped her head out of the trailer and whinnied.

Days have turned into weeks since we put Angel down. I took the time I needed to process what just happened. A lot of things were coming up for me. I realized that I had twelve years with Angel and twelve with my mom. My dear friend Judi who always rode Angel was born on the same day as my mom, July 7th. I mainly rode Nizhoni now. Daryl was too busy with restoring his classic cars. Over the past few years, it was Judi and I who were riding every week.

In a dream I had one night, my mom had impressed it on me that if she could be a butterfly, she could be a horse. I was really struggling with believing that my mom could have been Angel. The next day Judi came by and said she had something to show me. I was intrigued as I couldn't imagine what she was up to. She walked over to her car and opened the trunk. I looked inside and saw the most magnificent painting of Angel and Nizhoni. There was a big yellow butterfly near Angel and a poem about a Mother. I read the poem and realize it was my mom talking directly to me. A mom teaches her daughter how to face her fears and trust again after being hurt. Those are the things Angel taught me.

It didn't occur to me until later that if mom was Angel, I was with her as a woman looking into her eyes as she passed on to the other side. Maybe mom couldn't pass into her forever home until then. Only God knows. Isn't Life Grand, is what mom always said. She's right, Life is Grand!! It has been quite the ride.

ABOUT THE AUTHOR

I am amazed how far I have come. Death of a parent at 12, abandonment by the other parent at 15, and an early life of turmoil as a girl on the streets – running to find missing love and acceptance.

My journey has been exceptionally painful yet full circle - from hopelessness to a life filled with loving relationships. Over twenty-five years ago my life began to transform in so many magical ways. Wayne Dyer, sums it up well, *"If you change the way you look at things, the things you look at will change."* When you dream big dreams and reassemble a severely broken heart, your life can blossom into a blessed lifetime.

The magic dust which changed a dismal past into the incredible life I now live, is to believe that everything I hoped for was just ahead of me or perhaps it's realizing that everything I hoped for is actually here right now. I have learned to get out of my own way and to surrender to the will of God.

As a successful commercial property manager, I met my loving husband, Darek, and his two young sons. Now grown, our sons are building the life of their dreams, too. Darek and I are blessed to enjoy frequent travel; our homes in Colorado Springs and in Scottsdale with our sweet dog, Tinker; and two amazing horses that taught me the most valuable life lessons.

When you fall off, get back on, and go for the ride of your life!

Jennifer can be reached via email at: bothsidesnow1974@yahoo.com

Made in the USA
Coppell, TX
09 December 2020

43843698R00134